I Swear:
To Tell the Tooth

DR. CARROLL JAMES

ISBN: 1500648175
ISBN 13: 9781500648176
Library of Congress Control Number: 2014913481
CreateSpace Independent Publishing Platform
North Charleston, South Carolina

This book is dedicated to Karen, my loving soul mate.

Table of Contents

.

Prologue

"Wha'...what's happening?" Terrified, I shoot bolt upright. *It's just a dream, you idiot,* a small voice of reason answers from the fog deep within my brain.

But why does it happen so often? a louder, more urgent cry demands.

The dream—the nightmare—has followed me from childhood, through adolescence, and into adulthood. It won't let go. The nightmarish images, more vivid than reality, swirl like black-cloaked specters through my mind and soul. Has it foreshadowed my life? Maybe...probably. But my only true reality is the dream itself.

I'm ten years old—maybe eight or twelve. *Bonanza* is over and I've just donned my pjs, tired and ready for sleep. It feels good to close my eyes, yet I can still picture Hoss Cartwright riding the range, protecting the world from evildoers.

He crests the far ridge to disappear into the vastness of the American West, and a restlessness envelopes me. I'm left alone to patrol the range. The echo of pounding hooves fades in the distance; our house becomes almost too quiet. Everyone in my family has fallen asleep. My mind kicks into overdrive while myriad visions creep in to suffocate me in the darkness. My soul virtually tosses and turns to keep the world spinning in its proper orbit. It's my charge and…my curse.

In the dream, I'm in Grandpa's clapboard farmhouse, nestled against a hill up on The Ridge and being chased by someone who's laughing all the while. It's fun.

Quickly rounding the corner into Grandma's bedroom, I suddenly sense that it's not one of my mischievous cousins; or my sometimes diabolical brother; or even my crazy, senile grandfather. I catch a glimpse of a pointed black hat, and they don't wear pointed black hats. And it's not really a person—of that I'm sure.

The laughing abruptly stops, and I frantically duck into the only closet in the old farmhouse, one of those musty old closets that only has hooks along its shallow back wall. I can barely squeeze inside. With the door closed, it's darker than the black of a moonless Appalachian night with coyotes howling in the near distance.

Then it happens. My muscles tense as the horrid witch throws open the closet door. Although shorter than me, she looms larger in my mind, and hellishly ugly. Her mouth opens wide, spewing breath that reeks of putrid death. An evil howl emanates from the pit of hell. She lunges at me while her tongue rolls across jagged, scum-covered teeth. My heart pounds like a sledgehammer and I quiver uncontrollably.

Suddenly, I awake in a cold night sweat and find myself sitting upright on drenched sheets in my bed in Maryland, terrified of lying back down and closing my eyes.

It's sheer terror, the devil's work.

So…I decide to become a dentist.

One

THE DECISION

*I*s fear of dentists inherent in our DNA? In the movie *Marathon Man*, where a sadistic Nazi tooth carpenter inflicts horrifying pain, there were more audience groans and screams than in most slasher flicks. "No offense, Doc. Don't take it personally, but I hate the dentist." That's kinda hard to brush off after hearing it a few hundred times.

So why chose medical dentistry?

I enjoyed building models as a kid, was scientifically inclined, and excelled academically. My childhood dentist was caring and well respected in the community. Plus, he drove a cool car. But I could've become a vet or physician.

I once considered an appointment to the naval academy before attending a military high school where I bunked with five other guys in a room designed for two. The first night I went to bed homesick only to be awakened by a clanging bell and the boom of a cannon that shook the ancient windows. A bugler then screeched reveille. When the OD (Officer of the Day) burst into our barracks, he whacked my slow-to-get-up bunkmate with the side of his sword. Morning inspection was followed by company formation on the quad and marching to breakfast.

I quickly grew weary of that, but persevered through graduation.

My father constantly traveled for work, so he wanted to stay home whenever vacation time rolled around. But the summer of my sophomore year, Mom talked him into a trip to Niagara Falls. After several heated discussions, he acquiesced but with the condition that the trip be combined with business so the company would pay for it. When we got near Buffalo, we saw no roving buffalos. I was disappointed.

From Niagara, it was on to Watkins Glen where a delightful friend of Mom's had retired to a houseboat. While we relaxed lakeside, the friend suggested that a youngster might do well to consider a career in dentistry. "They don't work very hard and they make a lot of money."

Sounds good to me.

I began to daydream and pictured my dentist bounding into the hygiene room with an ear-to-ear grin for his cameo appearance after the pretty hygienist had done the *real work*. "How are things today, Carroll?" He'd plunge his fingers into my mouth and robotically mutter, "Fine, fine," before I could answer.

After poking around some, he'd declare: "Well, things look pretty good…only four cavities. We'll just fill 'em up and see you again in six months. Now be sure to brush *every* day."

Dad thought six-month checkups were just shy of highway robbery. "I'd like to sell shoe inserts to the same lady twice a year." He sported a full set of dentures. That summer I set my course.

On the way home, we swung by Lansing, Michigan, which was not really on the way, to fetch my grandmother from Aunt Aida's home.

Grandma had lived her entire life in the hills of southwestern Virginia, born and raised deep inside the magnificently wild, beautiful, and poverty stricken Appalachian backcountry. After Grandpa died she sold their ancient farm, which produced little more than rocks, and went to stay with her adult children and occasionally with her much younger siblings—nine of them, all girls. She'd be living with us for a spell.

After learning that her grandson wanted to be a doctor, that's all she talked about on the long ride back to Maryland. Mom couldn't contain her enthusiasm. "Can you believe it, Harry? Carroll's gonna be a professional!"

Dad mumbled something about eight years of college tuition. Born in 1899, he was quite a bit older than Mom and had never completed high school. As a self-made man, he had little use for *higher larnin'*.

I rode in the back of Dad's Buick, his pride and joy, which he'd never driven so fast. It was almost as if he was trying to outrun the shrill chatter coming from the backseat where Mom and Grandma sat. Although I was scared to death at the breakneck pace, my brother, Lee, sitting in the middle of the bench seat up front, seemed to enjoy it.

Safely back in Maryland, Grandma settled into the spare bedroom next to mine. After a hard life of struggling to make ends meet, she looked much older than her sixty-four years. A certain radiance, coupled with an ever-so-slight smile, brightened Grandma's withered face every time I mentioned college and dental school.

She loved spending time with her grandsons. There were no granddaughters. Lee and I would sit in her room, mesmerized by endless stories of "them ole days up on The Ridge." She related stories about the advent of electricity, the first car to make it up the treacherous mountainside, her only telephone (I do remember when the party line was installed), coal mine cave-ins, and, my favorite, rough-and-tumble altercations between *revenuers* and *moonshiners* as federal tax men searched for stills hidden in the dark recesses of those craggy mountains. I envisioned bloodhounds howling, feds shouting, branches breaking, and echoing gunshots before axes smashed into a wood-fired still, spilling white lightening onto the dirt.

On a crisp, yet sunny fall morning while I was getting ready for school, Mom called out. "Carroll! Go fetch yer Grandma. Breakfast is ready."

I knocked on her bedroom door: no answer. Gently pushing it open, I softly asked. "Grandma. You up?"

The room was dark and eerily cold. Her chamber felt of death, and I knew before I looked. Thankfully her eyes were closed; but had they been open, she would've been gazing heavenward. Grandma died peacefully in her sleep in the bosom of her family. She's buried next to Grandpa up on The Ridge.

Two

BEGINNINGS

The tumultuous sixties had come to a close by August of 1971 as the Vietnam War slowly stumbled toward an unresolved conclusion. After four years of premed, I arrived at Fairleigh Dickenson University in northern New Jersey along with a conglomeration of other professional wannabes. Most were from the parochial Northeast. In undergrad we'd been at the top of our class—the elite. That would change during the rigors of dental school.

At orientation, I became friends with a few guys with whom I grew closer to under the pressures of professional school.

Stan-the-Man was straitlaced and clean-shaven with short-cropped hair, black plastic-rimmed glasses, neatly pressed slacks, a starched button-down collar, white socks, and penny loafers. He'd emerged straight from the Buddy Holly fifties, totally bypassing the uniform of the sixties: bell-bottoms, sandals, and tie-dye T-shirts. His arms refused to swing when he walked, which gave him a dorky, robotic gait—easy to pick out in a crowd. Stan-the-Man spent that hot summer canvassing the urban landscape as a Listerine salesman and was quite adept at selling mouthwash to dentists, which foreshadowed his later success.

In decided contrast, goofy Gill sported the requisite beard, wire-rim glasses, and confident strut of the early seventies. His arms did swing rhythmically although he couldn't dance. But Gill didn't know that nor did he care. The school cited an obscure study about facial hair breeding harmful bacteria and pressured anyone with a beard to shave. Gill's wife recorded the traumatic sheering on silent 8mm film; you couldn't hear him weep, but I think I saw a tear. Being of Polish ancestry, Gill knew all the Slavic jokes.

Rock was rebel lite, like The Fonz on *Happy Days*; he was an unabashed free spirit. But unlike Fonzie, Rock already showed signs of male pattern baldness, which was accentuated by allowing his stringy hair to grow long, halfway down his back. Rather than garnering grief about hitch-hiking bacteria, he carefully rolled and secured his mane with pins to give it a short, trim appearance, which gave his sparsely covered pate a monastic look.

The school's dress code was a white lab coat over a dress shirt and slacks. And a tie, but they didn't specify what kind. Rock's only tie made psychedelic seem tame. Other than that, with his disguised hair he looked like a typical, mild-mannered dentist— by day.

Every morning, rain or shine, Rock rode a BMW muscle bike to school. When heading home, he removed the hairpins. With no confining helmet to tame them, those thin locks trailed freely in the wind. He took the narrow, winding mountain roads in northwest Jersey much too fast and once missed a curve, then launched handlebar deep into Lake Lackawanna. Rock replaced the ruined BMW with a tricked-out Harley.

The lovably rotund Floyd exuded an unkempt aura, like Pig Pen of Peanuts. At the Jersey Shore, Floyd had the whitest body on the beach. In order to burn evenly, he'd roll over in slow motion until he was bright red. Rock wryly declared, "You look like a beached whale."

Always smiling, Floyd's self-deprecating humor matched his sharp wit. He glanced up from his dime novel and grinned.

"Leave me alone; I'm protected by Greenpeace." Although no babe magnet, he did marry and later sired twins. Ironically, Floyd had only one testicle.

I was the middle of the road student who wore jeans and flannels or summer cutoffs and T-shirts when not in school. I shaved my college beard before Labor Day. My mild southern accent and down-home colloquialisms elicited grins and comments about my "hick roots." I considered nurturing this persona by wearing Grandpa's string tie, but then thought better of it. My friends treated me like a mascot from the planet Zork.

Our little clique didn't include any of the five females in our class. Women were just beginning to realize a long overdue equality in the American workplace. In a class of seventy-five freshmen, four of those five ladies were ordinary folk.

The fifth was not.

Disgustingly dirty, Ms. Oleander Jacob's foul body odor preceded her arrival; personal hygiene was nonexistent. She was well ahead of Floyd in grossness and he was too affable to be disgusting. Her unkempt clothes were not even stylish: a frayed wool poodle skirt and a heavy plaid vest. Along with combat boots and white knee socks, the ensemble looked way too hot for the last heat wave of summer.

In lab, our seats were alphabetically assigned like grade school. Accordingly, Ms. Jacob sat beside me for four long years. She lacked the *hands* (i.e., manual dexterity) to perform excellent, good, or even marginal dentistry. Students were paired with one another for clinical exercises, so I was inevitably yoked with "twitchy fingers" and squirmed in pain every time she practiced on me, her personal guinea pig.

"You're digging into my gums," I announced while she stripped off the top layer.

"They're all red. You have periodontitis," she said defensively.

"I taste blood." *I don't have gum disease; they're red because you're hacking at them.*

"Let me try again," she insisted.

7

Oh God. Let me die now.

A "practical" was a test using plastic mouths. There was a strict time limit and zero tolerance for inaccuracies. One such exam tested our didactic skills by having us fabricate a wax crown—a cap—on a plaster die we'd made previously. In private practice it's usually made in a lab, but we had to execute (Poor choice of words?) every step of the process. The wax was softened over an open flame and shaped with heated instruments.

Today was cap-carving time and students were understandably tense and jittery. The simplest mistake could be a major setback, leading to total failure. But prospective doctors need to become accustomed to the pressures of clinical practice.

It was unusually quiet as we filed into the bright lab; there was no bantering. We arranged instruments on cold, stainless-steel countertops that gleamed dispassionately in the fluorescent glare. Drawers and cabinets were yanked open, riffled through, and slammed shut while tense whispers drifted heavily through the sterile air.

"I've misplaced my wax instrument. Does anyone have an extra one?"

"I need a match. Anybody got a match? How 'bout a lighter?"

"Nobody smokes in here you nimrod."

"I'll bet Rock can scrounge one up. He smokes. Well, not cigarettes.

"Gotta fire up the propane somehow. But wait a minute; I can't find my Bunsen burner. Anybody seen it?"

There was a trace of desperation throughout it all. Several students would not be back the next year. A block of inlay wax, color coded so no one could sneak in a preformed crown, was distributed by the stern proctor.

As the wall clock's minute hand approached north, all became still and silent until the shrill clanging of the instructor's stop clock would herald the start. Clearing his throat with a solemn air, he announced, "The test begins…*screeeeech*…Now!"

Everyone buckled down to the task at hand while my heart skipped a beat. Sulfur matches sparked as the distinct *woof* of gas burners announced they were ablaze.

Oleander, seated immediately to my left, was more grimy-greasy-gross than usual. Her pungent odor mingled with the pervasive scent of cheap candles and the stifling heat of seventy-five miniature campfires. The mix began to weigh ponderously in the air, making the tension seem ever more onerous.

But wait! Something else is afire. A familiar stench?

Several nearby students raised their heads, sniffing the air like basset hounds.

Then it came to me: *Burning hair!*

My head instinctively snapped left in time to witness Ms. Jacob's hair burst forth in fiery glory. With mouth agape, I managed to stammer, "Oleander, you…you…your hair is on fire!"

She swatted at the top of her head absentmindedly, as one might at an annoying fly they have no hope of hitting. Irritated at the interruption, she briefly glared at me before bending back over the lab bench, pressing her chin firmly against her chest to look down through her coke-bottle eyeglasses. After all, the clock was ticking.

Not only had she failed to extinguish the blaze, but her flailing had further fanned the flames, which crept across her oily mop.

Floyd sat to Oleander's immediate left. He also noticed the flames and sprang into action, jostling his metal lab stool as he jumped up to grab a stack of paper towels beside the sink. He ran them under the facet and with the wet wad clutched firmly in his hand, dashed back and smacked her head. But his heroics merely created a breeze that encouraged the flames to further reach heavenward. Maybe it was my imagination, but I thought I saw a hint of blue. Was the conflagration going critical?

Maybe that student who couldn't find a burner could use Oleander's head.

Throughout it all, Ms. Jacob continued to work diligently; her detached, surreal countenance was in direct contrast to the flames shooting ever higher. Floyd and I had to do something about that blaze between us and soon. Using water to douse it wouldn't answer; grease lurked in the depths of her disheveled locks. Baking soda wasn't readily available, and the fire extinguisher seemed inappropriate. Then again, that might have been fun.

I stopped deliberating with myself and jumped up, knocking over my stool in the process. The steel crashed to the floor with a loud, metallic clang, which caught the attention of an ever-widening radius of students who now gazed wide-eyed at the pyrotechnic glory of Oleander the Human Torch. Filling a rubber mixing bowl with tap water, I flung it on her head. Miraculously, the flames were immediately extinguished.

But Oleander was drenched.

You might think she would've been grateful. Conversely, she could've expressed outrage that I'd soaked her. But she simply kept on working, never again raising her chin from her chest.

All the while, the instructor kept vigil by reading a cheap paperback. He briefly glanced up at the sound of my reverberating stool but remained clueless. Those students in the immediate vicinity of our little bonfire glanced around and grinned, enjoying the comic relief. Those seated further from the epicenter, unaware of the averted disaster, diligently carved their paraffin cubes without so much as pausing to see where the stench had come from.

With the head fire out, Oleander, along with the entire class, was safe from immediate harm. However, it was difficult for those few of us directly involved to concentrate. Furtively making eye contact, we quietly chuckled through half smiles. From time to time the proctor put his book down and strolled around to inspect our progress, never suspecting there'd been a close call in the "J" section. And she never acknowledged our help in rescuing her from a fiery death.

Everyone managed to pass that test, including Ms. Jacob and her fire brigade. The following day she arrived as slithery-slimy as ever, not having taken the time to wash her hair—forever true to form.

When she wasn't looking, I discreetly searched for a burned spot on her scalp but couldn't locate one. Somehow, the scorched area had simply blended in, disguised by the remaining grease. She looked up, caught me staring and actually smiled. I weakly smiled back, hoping that I wasn't sending the wrong signals.

Three

HOMER

"**Cadaver**: *n.* Latin: from *cadere,* to fall. A corpse, as for dissection; a dead body, especially of a person." From: *Webster's Unabridged Dictionary.*

"**24/7 Homer**: *n.* English: from cadaver, stiff, morgue meat. A Freshman's constant companion." From: The School of Dental Medicine.

How much information can be stuffed into the human brain? Take a wild guess, double it, and that's what you're expected to learn at dental school. The first two of four years covers basic sciences, especially Human Anatomy.

Cat anatomy in undergrad helped me prepare. For a whole semester I toted across campus a formaldehyde-saturated, half-butchered specimen stuffed in a clear plastic bag; the see-through bag was a nice touch. I spent hours in my Gettysburg frat house, hovering over a dead cat sprawled on the library table. My AXP Brothers protested:

"What's that awful smell?"

"Gross, Carroll."

"This library reeks."

"Do you really need to slice that thing up here? Man, I can't concentrate."

Despite the long hours, I found Comparative Anatomy fun and looked forward to human dissection where we first studied osteology—bones. In dental school, four of us were gathered around sixteen stainless-steel tables on which disarticulated human skeletons lay. It was the ultimate puzzle.

Tediously, we aligned each piece and memorized its physical properties: ligament and tendon attachments, grooves for blood vessels and nerves, cartilage articulations, load characteristics, etc. in preparation for dissecting a real human being. Well, a real dead one.

At the end of six weeks, we took a *practical* exam. Tags were attached to one part of a bone to be identified. When a bell rang, we moved bleary-eyed to the next table; not much fun at eight in the morning after yet another all-nighter. Coffee is a dental student's constant companion. But everyone was excited about the sixteen fresh stiffs that were coming next week.

That Monday morning I stopped in the lounge for the quintessential cup of high-test before catching the elevator to the second floor. When the door opened, the pungent stench of formaldehyde wafted down the hallway, overpowering the comforting aroma of my java. *Yep; this is the day of the dead.* When I opened the lab door, the malodor hit harder; eyes watered and sneezing became contagious among the students.

But through the tears, I saw no bodies; the dissection table's stainless-steel hoods, like on a backyard grill, were closed.

"Don't open them yet," announced the humorless mortician who we'd nicknamed Mort. "I want to go over a few do's and don'ts." He proceeded to drone on about the proper etiquette for slicing and dicing the deceased. "These people are just like you and me."

Rock snuck a quick peak under his hood. "They're not *exactly* like us," he whispered and grinned.

Mort glanced in Rock's general direction but continued: "Many donated their bodies to science. Others were homeless. Despite their humble demise, they also demand proper respect." Mort's monotone was sobering, especially his final admonition. "Anyone behaving inappropriately or making distasteful jokes will be asked to leave."

That got our attention. Being kicked out of lab, even for a day, would be a serious setback. You can't really stuff a cadaver into a clear plastic bag and drag it back to your apartment for study.

With a Ben Stein-like cadence, Mort announced, "You may now open the hoods and retrieve your dissection trays from the middle drawers." When the tops swooshed open, gags and gasps could be heard around the room. Oddly enough, I wasn't overly affected, probably inured to death by the shoutn'-'n-wailn' Nealy Ridge funerals of my youth. And the lab setting paled in comparison to finding my beloved grandmother deceased in her bed.

After dabbing formaldehyde tears from my eyes, I saw that the cadavers appeared less human, almost plastic, with no clothes and shaved heads. However, mine was definitely male.

The chief of human anatomy, who supposedly hailed from Argentina, strode into the lab and announced, "Ve vill start vit' ze scalp." His accent accentuated the macabre. It seemed doubtful that South America was his fatherland. "Please turn page t'ree of ze dissection manual." Edgar Allen Poe couldn't do it better.

Dissecting the scalp by carefully peeling back the skin took about an hour or so; not so bad. There's not much underneath except bone, and we were all familiar with bone.

But heading south was a whole different story. A person's face gives him identity, and cutting into it seemed like an invasion of his humanity; my stomach turned. I glanced around and saw that Stan and Gill were equally squeamish, having looked away from their respective tables.

The long, four-hour session was repeated three times a week for the remainder of the year. For a full month I couldn't eat meat. But given enough time, you can get used to anything. And it gradually became clear why Mort had hammered the rules. One way to deal with such a situation is to dehumanize it. We abided by the code of conduct—for the most part. But, without being disrespectful, we did add a light touch by naming the cadavers. Vinny, a member of my team, dubbed ours Homer.

"Homer?" I asked.

"Gotta call 'im something," Vinny declared.

"Yeah. But why Homer?"

"Why da hell not?"

Homer he was christened and Homer he remained. Actually, his full name became 24/7 Homer in honor of the amount of time we seemed to send with him. Only once have I spent that much time with another person. That was on my honeymoon and it didn't last a full year.

Pop quizzes became routine. Straining to read tags tied to sundry chunks of an increasingly desecrated body while racing Mort's timer after a good three hours of sleep became normal. While half the class rotated through the cadavers, the other half was sequestered in an oversized storeroom to await their turn.

The crowded storeroom held containers of various human parts. Anxious students rummaged through the stainless-steel jugs and crammed cabinets despite Mort's admonition "not to touch anything." His personal stash was forbidden fruit that we naturally wanted to pluck.

Leaning sleepy eyed against a fifty-five gallon drum in the corner, I inadvertently jostled the lid, which slid precariously but didn't topple off; I breathed a sigh of relief. Turning to investigate, Gill lifted the steel cover and lost his grip. It hit the tile with a clatter loud enough to wake the dead; and there were quite a few of them right next door.

Floating atop the liquid stench was one of Mort's weirder collections: bobbing eyeballs that stared lazy eyed and cross eyed and every which way.

"What the hell," Rock grinned.

"Why does Mort keep all these enucleated eyes?" Floyd wondered. There must've been hundreds.

I was trying to make sense of it when the door opened and Mort beckoned. "You guys are next," he said while stuffing a crème-filled donut into his mouth. Gill quietly replaced the lid.

As weeks progressed into months, the cadavers looked less human, which made the practicals ever more difficult.

"Was that thing on table four part of a liver?"

"Looked more like it's from a pancreas."

"It wasn't brain. Mort put them all into jars yesterday."

"Gross."

"And the eyeballs were removed from the storeroom." Rock sounded disappointed.

As winter gave way to spring, the intensity of freshman year got to everyone; the young, energetic students of autumn now dragged around in a fog. I found mornings particularly hard to cope with. To finish up the year, a major anatomy practical was scheduled that would decide whether or not we remained in school.

Everyone stayed up all night studying and it showed. Disheveled and disoriented, we drifted wearily up to the second floor, as if headed to our execution. Even the ladies hadn't bothered to primp. Oleander looked pretty much the same.

I smiled when I stopped at the first table. The Achilles tendon is nicknamed the *freshman ligament* because it's often misidentified. But I knew it, which renewed my confidence. The buzzer rang and I robotically moved through the familiar routine. After several stations, sleep deprivation again took hold.

But I was rudely jolted back to the land of the living at one table. The steel slab held a middle-aged woman with a full head of slightly gray hair. Only a small incision on the lower border of her right jaw marred her otherwise once handsome features. With her body covered by a surgical barrier, she seemed merely asleep and maybe a little cold.

I stared for the longest time. My introspective musings were suddenly broken by the piercing shrill of Mort's buzzer. I hadn't even looked at the tag. But it was too late; Rock was already shoving me aside. The one question I got wrong was one with which I should've been most familiar.

I later discovered that she was assigned to a graduate student who'd only begun dissecting her. Why her hair hadn't been shaved and why her skin hadn't had that pasty plastic appearance remained a mystery. At lunch, everyone was the talking about her.

"That lady looked so real."

"They're all real, you idiot."

"I'll bet you woke up in a hurry."

"More coffee's what I need to wake up."

"What say we sneak into the lab tonight and check her out?"

But we never did.

In our junior year, the pathology and anatomy departments collaborated, or conspired, on hospital rotations. Floyd, Gill, Stan, and I were assigned to assist autopsies at Belmopan Hospital on Manhattan's Lower East Side.

As with most hospitals, the dead were kept out of sight (bad press) and tucked away in the basement. We hopped a crowded elevator and Gill pressed B-4. The creaky old lift shuttered and jerked while dropping four levels. Mort might've liked the grave-like setting, but I preferred the second floor at school.

Spilling off the crowded elevator, we stopped to gawk at a line of recently deceased who lay face up on gurneys in the corridor, as if waiting to board the next boat across the river Styx. Harried hospital employees rushed past the gruesome queue as if it was normal. Floyd discovered a nondescript door about halfway down the hallway. "I think we're supposed to go in here."

Autopsy/Pathology Room B404.

"We're late; let's go," Gill prompted.

"I don't think the stiffs are going anywhere," Rock smirked.

The door creaked as it opened to a fetid odor that took my breath away. It was more than disinfectants or formaldehyde, although they were present in abundance. No, it was excrement, sweat, and…dust?

The chamber was stiflingly hot and crammed with people, most of them alive and sweating profusely. A hospital morgue usually has only two or maybe three autopsy slabs. Not Belmopan. Two rows of twelve tables each were jammed into a space designed for about ten; all were occupied while those corpses in the corridor patiently waited.

The sound of circular saws whirred above the general din. A short doc climbed onto a makeshift stepstool and tightly gripped a fat bone saw with both hands and removed the top half of a cranium. Homer's dissection had been more delicate with the small hacksaw-looking thing that we'd been issued. With twenty-four bodies in the room, at least one or two pathologists were always grinding away in a time when masks weren't standard. Several of them munched on donuts and bagels while coffee steamed lazily from mugs perched precariously on table edges. Their nonchalant demeanor helped me settle in to the surreal scene; but I could never bring myself to eat lunch in the cafeteria.

They asked us to consider the possible cause of death from only the gross evidence. The guy with his head half blown off in a botched gas station robbery was a no-brainer; we all got that one right.

I was absorbed in a case when Gill tapped my shoulder. I jumped. "Whadda you want, Gill?" He looked intense. "Carroll. You've got to come down to the far end of the room. A baby, just a few months old, aspirated milk. C'mon, the autopsy is just starting."

He seemed excited but my stomach turned. *There's a tiny baby in this bedlam?* I couldn't wrap my mind around it. *And what about the grieving family?* "That's OK. I'm plenty busy watching this."

Gill hurried away as I glanced down the macabre line of slabs. A tiny little body, the pinkness of new life replaced by a gray pallor, lay on a large, cold table. The law demanded an autopsy to rule out foul play. Fair enough, but it was more than I could handle, especially with the birth of my own son eminent; my eyes watered.

I never learned if the baby was a boy or a girl; didn't matter.

Each day in the morgue was a long one: twelve brutal hours that drained us physically and emotionally; but that first day seemed especially long. Upon leaving, we headed upstream past the endless parade of bodies lining the hallway. We paused when a gurney rolled past with an older man on it. He had a knife wound that traced a grotesque line across his neck. The police were in a hurry to learn the cause of death.

Stan pushed the elevator button when a loud commotion began in the adjacent stairwell. Through the door's window, we saw security guards restraining a middle-aged couple. The woman wailed uncontrollably while both of them struggled with the guards. "We just want to see our daughter!" the father shouted.

"I'm sorry, sir." The guard tried to be sympathetic.

"Sorry, my ass. Let me see our little girl."

Apparently their teenager had died of a heart attack while watching TV and was rushed to that gruesome place for a definitive diagnosis. Her parents, their faces contorted in anguish, simply wanted to be by her side. But the rules kept them out and that was a good thing; it was no place to say good-bye to a loved one.

We rode the elevator up and exited past the crowded desks in the lobby. I bumped into a young mother with dark rings around her reddened eyes. She was filling out forms. It was her baby who'd died of aspiration. The poor woman looked numb.

As the four of us hopped into my old, beat-up Ford Falcon, I wrestled with my emotions. The hour and a half ride back to Hackensack, New Jersey, was totally silent.

In our junior year we also started treating dental patients. It can take up to nine—that's nine—hours, over three sessions, for a student to complete his first filling. People suffer the long, multiple appointments because the cost was nominal and the work quite good, closely monitored by some of the country's best practitioners. I felt pretty good about my first one. It only took six hours over two sessions.

Although the patients knew, more or less, what they were getting into, even the most understanding people get antsy when trapped in a dental chair. Uptight parents trying to save a few bucks were especially aggravating.

My second patient was a very pleasant high school girl. However, her father was unlikable from the start. Slovenly dressed, with a three-day-old beard before it was stylish, he announced, "Do wha' ya gotta do, Doc. She don't 'preciate nothin' no how."

Ignorant rednecks in Joisey? Who knew?

I dreaded the moment when I had to tell him that she'd have to come back.

"Whaddaya mean? How the hell long is this gonna take?"

"I don't know, Mr. Sorrento. It depends on the instructor and how busy we are. You see, each step needs to be checked off and—"

"Jus' git it done quick like; no 'scuses, son." *Doc* had been replaced with a rather condescending *son*. I felt sorry for his daughter, who cringed and sunk slump-shouldered in the chair.

Before her second visit, I privately approached the instructor to explain the need to finish the case ASAP. "Is there any way I can get this checked off today?" Big mistake. Graduate professors are not known for their indulgence. He eyeballed me sideways and sauntered over to my chair in the middle of the large, open clinic.

"Shave about one-tenth of a millimeter off here and then we'll talk, Mr. James."

The old codger shuffled slowly away; a line of students trailed in his wake, like little ducklings. The clinic closed before he was again available. I placed another temporary filling and realized that my second restoration would take the proverbial nine hours. *Why on this yokel's kid?*

"Yer kiddin'? Look, I don't have time for this crap," Mr. Sorrento declared. "Her mamma's gonna have ta bring this sorry ingrate back; you be sure ta finish up next time or you got me to answer to." He pointed a finger.

Mamma has got be better than Dad. I was wrong.

She was coarser than the unsympathetic father. A guardian had to accompany a minor, but this lady wasn't about to stick around; she abandon her teenage daughter while I worked.

"Her dad will be back ta pick her up. I don't wanna fool wit' the little bitch. Eighteen won't come soon enough."

Dad showed up at the end, making a ruckus all the while. "Where's that little brat? How come she ain't waitin' fer me out front like I said?"

I had finished early, mainly because a more compassionate instructor was on duty. "She went to the lounge for a snack, Mr. Sorrento. I'll show you where that is."

"Make it quick. I got better things ta do than chase her sorry ass all around Bergen County," he growled while storming after me.

The poor girl looked mortified and quickly averted her eyes when he charged into the student lounge. "What the hell you doin' eatin' outta these expensive machines? We ain't made a money, ya know."

You would've thought that she'd just purchased a steak at Delmonico's. When he turned and stalked off, she started to follow but then stopped and timidly raised her head.

"Thank you very much," she whispered to me.

"You're welcome. You were a great patient."

She forced a slight smile before hurrying after her father. This poor girl had potential; she knew how to be appreciative. But her parents seemed determined to squash it before it could blossom. What a shame. What a waste.

My mind drifted back to the genuine grief that overflowed from that stark stairwell in the depths of Belmopan. Those parents of a daughter who died of a heart attack had a valid reason to make a scene. The lifeless infant lying on the sterile table loomed large in my mind, its poor mom in shock and disbelief.

If only the Sorrento's knew how blessed they were to have a child who was alive.

Four

KATE LEARNS TO ASSIST

Dad stared menacingly at me. "Why don't you get a job?" Nervous about the old man's continuing admonitions, I remained frozen to the kitchen chair.

"I graduated, Dad. But I still need a license in order to work."

"Humph," he grumbled before storming off, his bulldog head shaking.

Dad was a large man, still standing tall in his seventies. His dark hair was slicked back, accentuating his J. Edgar Hoover widow's peak. However, Dad never wore dresses; but he could still be scary. With no formal education beyond sixth grade, he felt that I'd been goofing off during my eight years of college and professional school.

The summer of '75 dragged well into its second month. At first I'd relished the free time, especially with my kids Tara and Russell. But they were often out with new friends or with their mom. After the rigors of dental school, their mom and I had grown apart. With the pressure of having no job, it was decided that we should separate, which ultimately led to divorce.

Now it was just me, and lazing around my parent's house all day had become tedious; I began to think Dad might be right. But what was I to do without a license to practice?

I spent a lot of time pacing. *I'm gonna wear a path in the living room carpet.* When I sat down to stare out the picture window, my leg began to jerk like a jackhammer. *Will I ever hear from the state board?*

On a hot muggy day in the month of despair, I saw the postman close our mailbox and ran down the driveway.

"Whoa there, Carroll. Looking for something?"

"Yes sir; maybe that brown envelope you just stuffed in there."

He pulled it back out and looked. "It's from the Maryland Board of Dental Examiners."

"Thank you, Mr. Cooley." I tore it open. *Congratulations Dr. James. You have successfully passed the Northeast Regional Board examinations.*

I smiled but then read farther: *Your records will be transferred shortly.*

Shortly! I needed those transcripts to apply for the jurisprudence exam. When they finally arrived a week later, I hand-delivered them to a nice secretary in Baltimore who allowed me to take the law test that day. I passed with 100 percent but still had to wait for more paperwork. And I had a family to support.

Between pacing sessions, I'd sent out dozens of job feelers, but no one wanted an *unlicensed* dentist. And Dad continued to think I was just freeloading. "Don't you think it's time you made your own way, boy?"

An oversized brown envelope finally arrived with a certificate embossed in gold lettering: **Carroll James, DMD**. The very next day a Dr. Dolph called me; things were finally moving along. He offered me an associateship, although we'd only spoken on the phone once. "Why don't you come in and look things over? See if you like my office."

I already knew I would like it. "Uh...yeah...great! When's a good time?"

"How 'bout tomorrow, say around five? And what kinda name is Carroll, anyway? Thought you were a girl." He didn't remember our conversation.

"Family name," I muttered. I'd been self-conscious about my name as a kid, but it's not all that unusual. The actor Carroll O'Connor comes to mind, as does my maternal uncle and namesake. I wanted to shout, "There's a Carroll County in Maryland." But I didn't. I just wanted a job.

Dr. Dolph's ground floor office was located in an upscale apartment building. A dark, solid door led from the main hall into a dimly lit waiting room with a high ceiling. The walnut paneled walls were lined with brown leather furniture that sat on murky, plush carpeting. Heavy drapes covered the floor-to-ceiling window. It had the feel of a Victorian library. Being a bookworm, I was impressed.

But I was more enamored by the buxom receptionist, immodestly attired in a low-cut blouse and tight chinos. Her perfectly straight, very white teeth—probably caps—brightened the dark room when she smiled. She moved like a Playboy Bunny, which I found out later she once was. "Can I help you?" She asked while provocatively leaning across the reception counter.

Flustered, I tried to look away. "Uh…I'm here to see Dr.… uh…Dr. Dolph."

"We're closing for the day." Her toothy smile faded to fake. Maybe like her chest?

"Oh, I'm not here for an appointment. Well…I guess I am. It's just that I'm looking for a job and—"

"Wait here." She and her smile abruptly disappeared.

Real smooth, Carroll. I'd been there only a few minutes and had already alienated Dr. Dolph's pretty receptionist who just wanted to go home after a long day's work. My palms felt clammy when he burst through the back door and exclaimed, "Good to meet you, Carl."

"It's Carro…Uh, nice to meet you, too," I stammered.

His overly tight tunic accentuated bulging muscles. Powerfully built with broad shoulders, the man obviously worked out. His firm grasp squeezed the wet from my hand, like wringing a dishrag. I wondered if I'd left a puddle on the floor.

A cursory tour revealed the lack of assistant stools, high-speed suction, or air-water syringes. The old office lacked any ergonomic design for modern sit-down four-handed dentistry. Elderly dentists could be easily spotted, shuffling along and hunched over like Quasimodo.

In contrast to his antiquated clinic, Dr. Dolph ran a dental maintenance organization, which was very novel at the time. He and his business partner employed 185 dentists who worked part time in their own offices for the DMO, although there was a full-time clinic in Dundalk. I didn't envision a future in mass-production dentistry but for now it would pay the bills, especially school loans. This would be a temporary situation until I could establish a quality private practice.

He did all the talking; apparently I was already hired. I would work two days a week for him with another day earmarked to start my own practice. Dr. Dolph's trusted assistant of many years, another trophy lass, would assist me. She didn't appreciate me showing her new techniques. "Well. That's not the way we do it *here*." Despite my advanced degree, I was on the bottom rung. After months of sporadic deliberations, Dr. Dolph reluctantly agreed to hire an assistant for me. I was thrilled.

Meanwhile, I'd gained his confidence as a clinician; he started to send difficult cases my way, especially DMO cases that had failed. And with a large pool of dentists, there was no shortage of botched work. But fixing a problem is not as hard as keeping the offended patient happy in the meantime. Dr. Dolph apparently thought I had an aptitude for this. Although I was well compensated, it was stressful work; especially when folks were spending an inordinate amount of time in the waiting room, which was always packed.

Dr. Dolph, making buckets of money on his DMO, lost all interest in private practice. His private patients were subtly thrown my way, lengthening my weekly hours. But that was a good thing; I needed the money. And although I had Mondays off, I frequently received an early morning phone call.

"Carroll." The receptionist never called me Dr. James. "You're needed here right away. Dr. Dolph (never Rolph) won't be in and the waiting room's already packed."

"You just found out?"

"He called in sick."

He wasn't sick; he just wasn't interested anymore. Almost every Monday I rushed out the door and arrived late to see irritated patients. After several weeks, I finally figured it out. I would shower and dress by 8:00 a.m., and then be ready for the inevitable call.

I now had my fledgling private practice, the remnants of Rolph's, and the DMO grind. From just a few hours a week, I worked six jam-packed days, one of which was a twelve and a half-hour marathon. The half-hour break for dinner on those frenzied Tuesdays seldom materialized. But I was young and motivated (i.e., broke). However, would my new assistant be able to keep up?

The happy answer was a resounding, yes! Kate's enthusiasm during her interview proved to be genuine. Her undying energy was more than a match for the grueling tempo. A fast learner with a pleasing demeanor, Kate was immediately liked by patients and she was efficient—a real plus for a young doc. Kate was a blessing.

Still, I'm not Superman and she wasn't Superwoman. "Even youths shall faint and be weary, and…utterly fall." (Isaiah 40:30.) Kate and I reacted to situations the same way: sometimes appropriately and sometimes…inappropriately.

When the rest of the staff left at five o'clock, we worked alone. Darkness fell early on one of those interminable DMO Tuesdays. I pulled back the heavy drapes and saw dark clouds rolling in. The drive home promised to be a bad one. But for now, we were running way behind.

"It's gonna be another late night, Kate." I'd caught a glimpse through the business office window of all the patients still waiting. Just then a middle-aged lady walked through the door with her unruly son in tow. Exhausted, I ducked into Rolph's private office for a quick break.

I had just slumped into his comfy desk chair when Kate came stumbling down the hallway and nearly fell through the door. At times she could be quite klutzy. But tears were running freely down her cheeks. Concerned, I sat bolt upright and asked, "What happened? You OK?"

She nodded her head yes while cupping her mouth in a futile attempt to muffle laughter. Her entire body convulsed as her free hand grasped the corner of the desk to steady herself. "Go look…check out…the reception window. You've got to see this for yourself." She regained some poise. "But be discreet."

"Right now?"

"Yes, now." She grabbed a Kleenex to wipe the tears.

I nonchalantly strolled down the hall and peeked around the corner. That adolescent had his bulging lips and bugger-encrusted nostrils plastered against the windowpane. Flanked by pudgy hands also pressing on the glass, his bug eyes quivered while a stream of drool trailed slowly down the window. He was panting like a basset hound trapped in a car on a hot summer's day.

Caught between this Dali-like vision and Kate's stifled, yet infectious laughter, I had no hope of maintaining decorum and beat a hasty retreat to Rolph's sanctuary. Kate followed hard on my heels. We shut the door, looked into each other's eyes, and burst into hysterical laughter. It was late, we were both exhausted, and…quite young.

Finally regaining my composure, I affected a serious "doctor" demeanor. But I couldn't look at her. "Kate, get Mom back right away. We're getting further behind."

"OK." She was also ready to go home.

Walking side-by-side, we turned the corner in tandem as the boy's lizard-like tongue flicked across the glass. I didn't need to glance at Kate to get her reaction; we made a quick U-turn and staggered back down the hallway, doubling over in fits of mirth.

"I…I'm glad that he's not on the schedule," I declared, wiping my eyes. "I'll stay out of sight while you seat her. Whatever you do, don't look directly at the window." Kate spit laughter through her nose before regaining her composure. She brushed back her hair and marched away, alone.

I practiced Zen-like breathing before entering the operatory. "Good evening, Ms. Jones. How are you tonight?"

She wasn't offended or rude or even nice. She showed no personality. *I wonder if she heard us.*

With reasonable self-control, Kate and I got down to the business at hand. Ms. Jones needed a white filling in her upper front tooth. I administered a local anesthetic and paused to let it work. An awkward silence ensued; the typical small talk was out of the question. I glanced in every direction except Kate's.

Although I'd developed a certain confidence in her, Kate still required close supervision. She was a quick study, but her training wasn't on holiday.

In order for me to see behind the upper front teeth, an assistant had to blow air over the mirror, which otherwise fogs. A good four-handed assistant also used her air/water syringe to wash the prepared cavity before I filled it.

"OK, Kate, now dry the tooth."

She confidently rotated the angled tip, aimed it upward, and…missed. Compressed air shot up Ms. Jones's nose, her nostrils billowed like a blowfish from the blast. Kate gasped in horror while the lady's eyes bulged; they looked like her son's.

Unable to hold it in, Kate began to rock with laughter. It was a miracle that she didn't fall off her stool and onto Ms. Jones. But her reaction was infectious; I spewed laughter, which I tried to disguise as a cough. "Excuse me, Ms. Jones."

Ms. Jones saw no humor in it.

After we finished up, she made a beeline exit and grabbed her son's hand on the way through the waiting room. She didn't pause to look back. But he did, pressing his chubby face against the glass one last time. His tongue lashed out and quickly drew back, as if he'd caught an insect. Mom yanked him out the door.

Kate and I degenerated into hysterics. Those patients still waiting must've wondered what was so funny. Maybe they just thought we were a happy team. They would've been right.

The following day, I spent extra time reviewing basic technique with Kate, dwelling specifically on the air/water syringe. Yet the phrase, "Dry the area" still evoked a slight grin and comic relief on particularly tough days.

Yup, Kate worked out just fine.

I even married her.

Five

MᴵL

"Nuthin's stronger than blood." Clan loyalties can be fierce in southwest Virginia where my mother hails from. For generations, the Arringtons farmed rocks about forty miles from Tug Valley, the epicenter of the infamous Hatfield and McCoy Feud. But back in Maryland, loyalties were sorely tested when I fished for patients. The family discount didn't get any bites; relatives knew too much about my oft times mischievous youth. More on that later.

Mischievous. I always thought it meant harmless fun. But in *Webster's 1828 Dictionary*, the word is defined as *harmful; hurtful; injurious*. Although I intended no harm with my childhood pranks, they now seemed to matter. We were talking about the dreaded dentist.

"Sooo…Carroll. How's it goin'? I'd make an appointment, but I've already got a dentist."

"Keeping busy in Dr. Dolph's fancy office?"

Cousin Clyde was the straight shooter. "Been sued yet?" Having moved to Northern Virginia for a job, Clyde sported a removable partial denture to replace two front teeth lost in a bar fight. "But you oughta see the other guy."

When I asked if he wanted a new partial he said, "It fits just fine, Carroll." But it didn't. Clyde seldom wore it but didn't want me "foolin' 'round in his mouth." He once saw me and my cousins blow up an outhouse.

Although he'd been anxious for me to get a job, Dad never came in for an appointment. Lacking any teeth, he had recently been fitted with new dentures. He'd forgotten that he could've gotten a freebie. Or maybe he didn't trust me either.

Mom boldly made an appointment for a cleaning. Maternal pride over sanity? A tough mountain woman, she didn't seem at all nervous—at least she didn't show it. That prompted a second cousin twice removed along with a few friends to slowly drift my way. But most kept an ear cocked for any blunders.

"Been to Carroll's office yet?" the first cousin asked.

"No. But my wife's cousin tried him out," the second cousin replied.

"Any screw ups?"

"Nope; she's still alive."

"He expensive?"

"He's a dentist."

To her everlasting credit, my mother-in-law, with no blood obligation, scheduled a checkup soon after Kate and I wed. Jean was Arkansas Ozark, close enough to Appalachian; I was anxious to make a good impression. But it's hard to screw up a cleaning; pretty basic stuff. My game plan was to be friendly and caring, all the while maintaining a professional demeanor. No joking around.

Jean was fastidious about brushing and flossing with only a few tiny fillings from years ago; never any major work like root canals, caps, or gum surgery. Toward the end of the visit she mentioned one minor complaint.

"Carroll…uh, *Dr.* James," she said with a grin. "I hesitate to even bring it up, but a molar has been aching on and off. It's probably nothing."

Uh oh. I didn't see that coming. "Which one, Jean?"

"Right here; toward the back on the top left," she said while stretching her cheek. Jean was no complainer and only brought it up as an afterthought.

I affected a pensive attitude and poised my pen over her chart. "Does it hurt when you chew?"

"Not necessarily."

"Okay, what about hot or cold?" I recorded her answer.

"No." She was definite.

"Does it get worse when you lie down? Or—"

"I haven't noticed anything like that, and—"

"Does it ever wake you up during the night or keep you from going to sleep?"

"It's not been that bad."

Ice, heat, and percussion didn't hurt. Radiographs at various angles revealed nothing. My standard repertoire led nowhere. I could find no cause for her intermittent *discomfort*; dental-speak for pain. However, her chart was now full of illegible scribbling. Surely that was impressive.

"It sometimes aches for no apparent reason and quickly goes away," she volunteered.

"Ahhh!" I said, as if I'd had an epiphany. A vague, nonde-script twinge suggested a simple bruise, which folks can seldom pinpoint. However, Jean consistently pointed to the same tooth. I probed deeper.

"You're digging into my gums, Carroll!" So much for Dr. James.

It wasn't going to be an easy diagnosis, but I had to say something definitive. After all, I was the sharp young doctor trained in the latest techniques. "Maybe additional symptoms will come to light if we give it more time." Time was the quintessential medical cop-out.

She stared at me as if to say, *This is the best you can come up with?*

I was confident that there was no infection and didn't want to rush into treatment. "Promise me that you'll report back right away if new symptoms develop. It's vital to know exactly when or if it takes a turn for the worse." Lame.

She agreed and, if nothing else, appeared satisfied with my non-advice. "Thank you," she said with a smile upon leaving.

But I wasn't satisfied. The easy "everything is fine, see ya in six months" checkup I'd hoped for had failed to materialize. Then again, maybe I was right and it was a simple bruise; I'd look the hero when it went away. Fat chance! St. Apollonia, the Patron Saint of dentists, wasn't going to let me off that easy.

On a crisp autumn afternoon, Kate and I drove over to my in-law's home for Sunday supper. The sun's warm rays filtered through the shimmering red and gold of the maple trees, lending a pastoral air to the Lord's Day. Jean's cheerful greeting glowed warmly, reflecting the stand of burning bushes behind their brick home. "Come on in. Frank's in the sunroom watching football, Carroll."

"Thanks. Something sure smells good." I smiled and headed for the enclosed porch around back and plopped down on the couch as the second half of the Redskins game began. I asked Frank, Kate's dad, "So, whose winning?"

"The Skins. Who else?"

Stupid question; Joe Gibbs was coaching, so of course they were winning.

Frank grabbed a handful of beer nuts and chased them with a pull on his scotch and soda. Kate's mom promptly showed up with a beer, the perfect complement to the chips and salsa she placed on the coffee table. Dinner would have to wait until the game was over.

It was worth the wait. The Skins won. After dinner, Jean, ever the gracious host, subtly got up to clear the table. "Everyone just stay put while I tidy up a bit. I'll fetch desert shortly."

Although Frank was antsy for her warm homemade pumpkin pie à la mode, she served me first. I dug in and had just stuffed my face when she paused by my chair, balancing several serving plates in her hands.

"You know, Carroll; that tooth is still the same."

I tensed as a large chunk of pie—humble pie—squeezed down my throat and landed in my stomach with a thud. I put my fork down and looked up. "That's a shame, Jean. Call the office tomorrow morning; we'll take another look." I stared down as my ice cream melted soupy over the hot piecrust.

Frank quickly polished his off. "You going to finish yours, Carroll?"

"Nah. I'm stuffed." I shoved it over and he gobbled it up. His slight frame belied a healthy appetite; the man could eat anything and not gain a pound.

Jean popped into the office later that week. *Something must've changed for her to bring it up at supper,* I mused. *This could be a good thing.* That was not to be.

I probed and prodded and found nothing. A follow-up radiograph proved worthless. Her answers were verbatim to my progress notes. But I had to do something.

"Jean, has the pain gotten more intense?"

"Not really."

So why'd you bring it up over dessert? "Let's give it a little more time." I tried to sound sincere.

She knew that was a cop-out. But her smile, a beacon of graciousness, made me feel that much worse. She returned a couple months later for her six-month checkup with the same impeccable home care; no cavities or gum disease.

"Everything's fine, Carroll. Well; that one little thing still bothers me."

Oh God, no!

That wayward tooth had continued to act up without getting any better or worse. "Time" hadn't done the trick. Another radiograph (*Is this three or four?*) yielded absolutely nothing. I almost hoped to see an abscess. At least then I could treat it. As I had been in practice for only a short time, I probably looked naïve or incompetent. I certainly wasn't making any points with my young bride.

I guess it's called practice because you never quite get it right. What had I overlooked?

"Let's try an oral rinse and nutritional supplements, along with a regimen of broad-spectrum antibiotics for that low-grade sinus infection."

What sinus infection?

Without questioning the wisdom of my shotgun approach, Jean cheerfully agreed. I reasoned that if it was psychological, a placebo just might do the trick. Only time would tell. But so far, *time* hadn't worked out so well.

That afternoon, Kate asked, "What do you think about Mom's tooth?"

"Well…" I reluctantly related myriad diagnostic possibilities along with my proposed non-treatment, treatment. "Honestly? I don't know if it'll work." I felt defensive. "Look, Kate. It might've been a real pain at first. But it's probably all in her head now."

That was a huge mistake. Husbands can be so dumb. Kate shot me a piqued look, but I continued to dig a hole. "A lot of things are psychosomatic, you know."

Kate's whole body tensed as her eyes narrowed.

I totally misread her, thinking that my medico-technical jargon had impressed her. I had yet to learn that Latin never really makes a doctor look good. "Even if it was a hyperemia—that's a bruise, Kate," I said condescendingly, "it has evolved into a ghost pain that's stored in the cerebral cortex as leftover baggage." I was sort of happy with the way I'd handled it.

Kate, on the other hand, was way beyond insult. She firmly planted her hands on her curvy hips and leaned toward me, somehow appearing taller. "Are you suggesting that my mother is a basket case?"

"Uh, no. I just thought—"

"Do you honestly think all women are ditzy?"

A collision was in the making. It was time to backpedal. "Well, no. This might…uh, does happen with men as well." But instead of leaving it there, I continued. "I don't think it happens as often with men." What the hell was I thinking?

Mark Twain once said, "It's better to keep your mouth shut and appear stupid than open it and remove all doubt." Good advice.

My aggrieved, agitated spouse spewed a series of abusive epithets, none of which I can remember. And if I could, I couldn't repeat them. I looked for cover, but saw nowhere to go. An honest defense had been tried and found wanting. Tired and frustrated, I blurted, "Your mother is *simply neurotic*! There's no other explanation."

If you've never experienced the icy silence of a wife scorned, try dissing her beloved mom. Too late, it dawned on me that I'd committed a serious breach of mother-in-law etiquette. I felt blood draining from my face while Kate stormed off. Her cold shoulder continued throughout the afternoon, and she spoke not a word during the long ride home.

After a lonely dinner of PB&J, I went out back and read until late, then crept into bed once Kate was asleep. It took several days for things to thaw.

Several months elapsed and I'd almost forgotten the whole thing when I saw Jean's name posted on the day schedule: TA–toothache. Kate had also highlighted it with a red Sharpie.

Oh no! A cloud of gloom slowly enveloped me as the day dragged on. When it was her appointed time, I ducked into my private office to call an oral surgeon. It was a delay tactic; I could've done that anytime.

Kate seated her mom while I cowered in my office. I hung up and thought about hitting the head. *Can't put this off forever, Carroll.* Slump-shouldered, I shuffled into the operatory wishing I was anywhere but here.

"Good afternoon, Jean," I muttered sheepishly.

She tilted her head up toward me and presented with the sweetest countenance you've ever seen while pointing to her left cheek. I bent over and saw that the inner wall of the upper first molar—our old friend—was gone. My mouth dropped slack-jawed as Jean retrieved a folded tissue from her purse. "I was wondering if you needed this." It was the jagged piece of tooth that had sheared off.

"No." *Not really.*

A microscopic fracture had caused her pain from the get-go. "A hairline fracture is impossible to detect clinically," I babbled, "even with radiographs. No way to know until it actually breaks…" and so on.

She continued to smile throughout my meanderings but really just wanted it fixed.

"Let's smooth it off for now," I offered. After I filed it down, an uncomfortable silence ensued, which I decided to fill with more inane rambling. "Happens all the time you know. Teeth chip for no apparent reason."

Kate stood in the background, shaking her head. I had to do something to assure them both that I knew what I was doing. "After it's properly restored with a crown, the sensitivity will abate and you'll be able to eat normally." I hoped.

When I stopped to take a deep breath, Jean proclaimed, with a twinkle in her eyes, "You see. I'm not *neurotic!*"

Blood again drained from my face as I realized that Kate had told her what I'd said in frustration. Weak-kneed, I plopped onto my stool as I realized that Kate told her mother *everything.*

And from that day forth I have never, ever—even jokingly—referred to any patient as neurotic, but especially not kinfolk!

Six

THE HANDWRITING ON THE WALL

Dr. Dolph was so angry when I gave him notice (three months), he fired me from the DMO and wouldn't let me finish work I'd already started on my patients. Homeless, I frantically searched and found a new, unfinished medical building. But it would cost a lot to complete my suite. Money, again, became an issue.

I had to pay the landlord, architect, banker, accountant, lawyer, plumbers, electricians, carpenters, etc. And the federal, state, county, and city fees were exorbitant, along with large deposits to utility companies. Equipment, instruments, and professional supplies were the final budget busters. Second-hand furniture would have to make-do for now.

And there were never-ending hassles with chronically late workers and shoddy work. But it slowly came together until a few disgruntled neighbors cast a pale.

Early one morning I arrived at the building to find an eerie stillness; there was no construction noise, not even a hammer pounding. Inside I found a red-lettered notice posted on the door of my almost completed office. "All construction is prohibited until further notice." The patients we'd already scheduled would have to be postponed—indefinitely. Hope faded.

Those residents who'd complained about a commercial facility noticed that the handicap access didn't satisfy updated codes. The landlord applied for an exception, but that takes time. Our small patient base dissipated into the ether. Not that I could blame them.

Miraculously, the work stop order was soon lifted and my dental chair was installed. Things were looking up as my brother, Lee, and I unloaded used waiting room furniture from his pickup.

I was eager to deliver the high-quality treatment I'd dreamed of, but there was still one thing missing: patients. Surprisingly, a few loyal folks had hung in there but not enough to pay the bills, including those staggering school loans.

And those high-tech telephones that I'd spent so much on didn't seem to work, a multiline/multifunction setup foisted on me by a slick salesman. In my frustration, I envisioned stringing a phone cord around his scrawny neck. I had Kate call from home as a test; they rang as promised. It was just that no one was calling. Then it rang again. I became excited until I realized it was Dominoes offering two-for-one pizzas at lunch. I couldn't even afford that.

I tried a couple of publicity stunts that went nowhere and advertising was considered beneath a doctor's dignity in the 1970s. Although I remained adamantly opposed to DMOs, especially after the unethical practices of my former boss, something had to be done.

For short stretches I was busy enough to keep my head above water. Then the phones would again go on strike. Casework was lucrative but scarce; what I needed was a consistent patient flow. As the roller-coaster ride continued, melancholy gave way to depression and I began pacing like I had when waiting for a license.

The trade journals were full of articles by gurus who promised, "Ten *Easy* Steps to Attract Twelve New Patients a Week." Never happened, but I did manage to spend a lot of the bank's money on various subscriptions.

Although Kate remained upbeat—a Pollyanna to my Eeyore—my mood didn't improve when classmates bragged about their booming practices. I consoled myself with the knowledge that they'd joined numerous dental plans. Of course they were buying homes, taking exotic vacations, and eating real food while I stalked in circles and lost weight. But "All good things come to those who wait." *Yeah, right!*

During the slow periods—most of the time—I retreated to my private office to brood in solitude. With a heavy heart, I'd plop my butt down on the soft leather chair behind my oak desk. Very expensive; they were the only furnishings I hadn't skimped on.

I wrestled with confused emotions. *What was I thinking when I went into dentistry?* I'd remember the pride on Grandma's face. And new patients were always an emotional lift. Chatting about spouses, children, pets, and homes would always pull me out of the doldrums. But I quickly regressed when I had too much time to fret.

One day, while sitting alone in my office, Kate rudely disturbed my sulking by barging in to find me slouching behind my desk. She hadn't even knocked before sailing past the distinctly marked Private sign.

"Isn't it obvious I don't want to be disturbed?"

She tried to lift the pervasive gloom by cheerily announcing the latest news from the front desk. "The afternoon patient just canceled. You can take a break."

A break! I steamed without saying it. *A break from what?* The whole day—the whole week—had been free time. And this wasn't just any cancelation; it was an extensive case that I'd counted on to pay some overdue bills. In no frame of mind to be cheered up, I growled, "Leave me be."

Proudly displayed on my desktop was an elegant ballpoint pen and classic fountain pen mounted in a marble base. The set had been presented to me by Kate's aunt at our grand opening. A celebration that now seemed premature.

Fountain pens have a little lever on the side to suck ink from an inkwell bottle. That archaic device is seldom used today. Only a skilled calligrapher can properly wield it without trailing ink all over the paper. With too much time on my hands, I had repeatedly pumped the lever, loading it to the max.

Kate was determined to keep me from sinking further under. An exaggerated frown wrinkled her pretty face as she snatched the fountain pen to make her point. "You need to lighten up, Carroll," she teasingly scolded as her wrist crisply flicked the pen for emphasis.

A jet-black stream shot from the slotted tip, streaking my forehead, spectacles, cheek, chin, and neck. The black line continued down my shirt and left a speckled trail across my brand new highly polished desk.

I sat stunned while a smudge drifted slowly down one eyeglass lens, distorting Kate's figure, as if I were looking at her through a glass darkly. She gasped. With my unobstructed eye, I saw a look of horror spreading across her fair visage.

In a clumsy attempt to recover, she snapped her wrist in reverse, whipping the pen upward to deliver a second line across the desk, my body, and the other lens. The momentum continued skyward to trace an ever-widening stripe of black goo up the freshly painted wall and onto the ceiling.

Through the two oozing blobs of India ink, I could barely see Kate covering her mouth, surely mortified at the mess. Knowing it was an accident, I tried to remain calm and slowly removed my spectacles. Then I saw that, instead of being horrified, she was actually covering her mouth to stifle a laugh. But she managed to gurgle, "I think I'm going to wet my pants!"

No longer able to contain herself, she squealed and bolted for the restroom, holding her sides all the while. "I'm so sorry." But I don't think she was. She knew I needed a good laugh in the worst way. And the worst way was how I got it.

That's when the humor of it dawned on me. Kate's stifled reaction was infectious. Although I tried not to crack a smile, her shenanigans were like a refreshing breeze in the midst of summer doldrums.

She returned with a handful of tissues and tried to clean my face, which further smeared the goop. I cleaned my glasses and grinned sheepishly, but still couldn't bring myself to laugh out loud.

The lesson was more than a few dabs of splattered ink. Kate unwittingly got me back on my feet. There's more to a person's overall well-being: love, joy, and of course, laughter. Too often these are found wanting. *Stuff* will never satisfy, which I rediscovered in the midst of unproductive worry.

Business eventually picked up, became very successful, and personally satisfying. That broad band of ink on the ceiling has faded, but it's still there. Whenever life's pressures start to get me down, all I have to do is lean back and look up. A slight grin will creep across my face. Sometimes I chuckle softly.

However, I've never refilled the fountain pen.

Seven

DR. FRIEDEN

My buddy Stan couldn't believe his horned-rimmed eyes. His new fifty-pound X-ray head drifted down onto his patient's lap and pinned him to the dental chair. Stan pulled while his elderly patient frantically pushed. With the help of his petite assistant, they wrestled it to the floor.

Although Stan's equipment was state-of-the-art, his construction had been done on the cheap. He'd hired a friend to convert the neglected half of an ancient ranch house into his office. The other half housed an Italian restaurant. The kitchen divided the two halves. Patients could have dental work and pasta with a glass of merlot.

His erstwhile handyman had announced that the walls were "good 'n' strong. Jus' need a little dressing up is all." When the heavy X-ray head was extended to take a film, it put incredible strain on the walls. Stan's walls had ballooned like an aneurysm.

Thankfully, the patient was a friend with a good sense of humor. Stan gave him a discount and didn't charge for the radiographs.

A few years later, his practice had grown exponentially, forcing him to move to a new location. He hired a bonded carpenter who grandly proclaimed. "I got this place built like a fort. Them studs is equal to the task."

Stan's second opening day found an unwitting patient firmly pinned to the chair by the X-ray. Late-night wrestling isn't this predictable. The victim was the same old guy as before. Stan gave him another discount.

So when I located to an upscale suburb, I was determined to avoid a structural mishap. I told my carpenter to beef up the walls with double two by eights.

He argued with me. "That's overkill. You trying to shore up the Bay Bridge?"

"Yes," I insisted. I've had no crushed patients to date.

As Minor Medical Building neared completion, the landlord radically raised the rent on the few unleased suites. Dr. Frieden, also a dentist, got the last one, which was across the hall from mine. The construction noise, which had only recently been music to my ears, would soon pass.

Dr. Frieden, well into his fifties, had always worked for the government or one of those storefront chains that were popping up like weeds. He'd decided to try private practice, but time wasn't on his side. It takes youthful energy to launch this backbreaking business. And it would be at the expense of second and third mortgages on his home. But he was undaunted.

Too soon, the noise ceased and a shingle proudly hung on his door: *Dr. Frieden, DDS.* Moseying over to meet and congratulate him, I found his office locked but later ran into him in the parking lot.

"Hi, I'm Carroll James."

"Glad to meet you," he said and smiled gregariously. "I'm waiting for an occupancy permit." *I know that song.* "Should be open in a day or so." *You hope.*

"Looking forward to seeing your suite," I said with encouragement.

He soon got the permit, but I never saw any folks going in or out of his office. His patient base had to be even smaller than mine.

Minor Medical was in a residential neighborhood shaded by ancient oak trees. My office looked out back on the tenant parking lot. The asphalt wasn't picturesque, but the view of the homes was better than Dr. Rolph's non-view had been. Gazing outdoors is a nice break from dentistry's cramped venue. Yawning mouths and sterile walls can be a bit claustrophobic.

On one bright, cheery day while my patient was rinsing, I glanced out at the squirrels scampering along the privacy fence and saw portly Dr. Frieden standing motionless in the parking lot, his silhouette reminiscent of Alfred Hitchcock. He was catatonically focused on the trunk of his old beat-up car; the fenders and door panels were different colors with primer gray as the prevalent mood.

He became suddenly animated and slammed his fist on the trunk; the tired old hinges groaned as the battered lid struggled to open. Then he again stared statuesque into its depths. After what seemed an eternity, he reached into the trunk and retrieved a weather-beaten golf bag. The old clubs might've fetched a pretty penny from an antique dealer if they'd been in decent shape. They weren't.

I mechanically holstered the drill and leaned back to watch as the open-air drama developed. My patient had finished rinsing and asked, "What's up?"

"Dunno. Check out the parking lot; see if you can figure it out."

Dr. Frieden dug out an old golf ball that sported a number of smiley faces carved by a club. He placed it directly on the hard pavement and threatened a practice shot that invited destruction to the club.

Anticipating a *coup de grace* for the aging equipment, my patient, an accomplished golfer, leaned forward to watch. He, Kate, and I tensed as the doc twisted slowly into a perfect backswing. Reversing in slo-mo, he swung an unblemished follow-through without hitting the pavement.

He took a half step forward and formally addressed the ball.

"Uh oh. He's actually gonna hit it this time," I muttered. But he didn't move. He looked like Lot's wife after gazing back at Sodom and Gomorrah.

After the salty interlude, Doc Frieden gently tapped the ball, which rolled under the car. He placed a protective sock over the club head (it might've been a real sock) and gently placed the cracked leather bag back into the trunk. He was a cheerful diversion during my day.

I later discovered that his waiting room was early flea market, like the golf clubs. A couple of old wooden chairs sat on a myriad of carpet samples; unsightly concrete floor showed through the gaps. The motley assortment of colors, designs, textures, and patterns—blue, green, red, yellow, mauve, checked, striped, spotted, and plain—lent a chaotic, Wonderland-like aura.

I searched the room for a reception window and discovered only a simple door with the same monochrome paint as the walls: autumn wheat. I tripped on an exposed edge of the Byzantine floor. To avoid any more pitfalls, I stepped high like a Lipizzaner. There should've been a sign on his door: ENTER AT YOUR OWN RISK.

I knocked softly. No response. I rapped a little louder, and still no response. My imagination took flight, half expecting a large white rabbit to pop up from the animated floor. *Guess he's not in.*

As I turned to leave, the door suddenly flew open. Standing in the entranceway sporting a broad smile was a balding, five-foot-ten rabbit in a white tunic. I shook my head to refocus on Dr. Frieden.

With a firm handshake and hefty slap on the back, he greeted me. "Come on in, Carroll. Glad you could stop by. I've seen you through those nice big windows. You're pretty busy."

I hoped he hadn't noticed us staring at him. "Jus' wanted to say hi."

"Wanna take a tour?" He was obviously delighted with his accomplishment.

"Sure. I'd love to."

The tricky terrain continued within. When I again tripped on a remnant, he caught my arm and smiled. "Watch your step, Carroll."

His only treatment room was straight back. I looked in and thought, *Is this a family room or an operatory?*

An old console TV, shoved against the near wall, had been conscripted as a countertop. There were far too many instruments piled on the faux-wood top. I eyeballed the large knurled on-off knob to the right of the semi round screen and considered pulling it just to see if the TV worked. Upon more sober reflection, I decided not to; the sonorous **click** might've sent instruments tumbling to the floor. The room smelled musty and I squeezed my nose to forestall a sneeze.

The dental chair was operated by a pump-action foot pedal. It resembled an old barber's chair except for those little black round things to trap a patient's head. The seat cushion had a strip of fabric tape on it. At least it wasn't duct tape.

The porcelain cuspidor—spittoon—was the size of a birdbath. I imagined the bulky freestanding X-ray machine emitting crackling sounds reminiscent of Dr. Frankenstein. If it were to fall, like Stan's had, it would surely kill. The archaic belt-driven drill did promise to vibrate a patient half to death.

It was all reminiscent of the 1950s; too recent to be antebellum, but not old enough to be quaint. And there was no sink.

The only place to wash hands or instruments was down the hall in the lavatory. That washbasin was ringed with instruments while another pile sat on the back of the commode. I wondered how a modern professional could practice in such a disorganized, bacteria-friendly venue. Then again, he didn't work all that often. It's safe to say that he didn't have an equipment mortgage.

"Thanks for showing me around, Doc. It's real…nice. I'd better get back. I've got a patient due about now," I said. It was a white lie.

"Good for you. Stop in anytime."

I carefully negotiated the moonscape to get out.

A particularly gloomy, rainy day rolled around in late November. The Christmas and New Year holidays were approaching, which made my schedule lighter than usual. It'd been a while since I'd last called on the old golfer, and I hadn't seen him in the parking lot, especially now that the cold weather had set in.

Cheerful despite the weather, I carefully walked into his waiting room but avoided looking at the vertigo-inducing carpet; I'm prone to motion sickness. The inside door was slightly ajar. I pulled it farther open and softly called, "Doc, you back here?"

There was no answer, so I spoke a little louder. "Hello. Anybody home?" It was quiet—too quiet. Not a soul was in the operatory/family room. To the right, the storage closet was closed, but to the left the bathroom door stood wide open. I saw a pair of bony knees with polka dot boxers draped around ankles. The polka dots matched the age spots on his legs. Dr. Frieden sat calmly on his porcelain throne, absorbed in a magazine propped on his lap. He was unaware of my presence; anyone could've ventured in.

I quietly backed away, fled across the hallway and stumbled into my lab while bursting out laughing. Kate came running.

"You OK?"

Punch-drunk, I tried to describe the privy scene to which I'd just been privy. "He's just sitting there…humming…polka dots…"

Kate's sideways folded arms and her look implied that I must be exaggerating.

"Go see for yourself." Tears streamed down my face.

"I'll pass." She realized I couldn't have made up something that absurd.

Arriving for work on a crisp winter morning a couple months later, I squeezed my car past a moving van parked out front. Two burly tattooed men struggled to lift a heavy, out-of-date dental chair over myriad carpet samples scattered on the truck floor. Standing beside it with his eyes downcast and shoulders slumped, Dr. Frieden mumbled, "I'm gonna retire."

He was a nice guy, but he made the right decision.

I do hope he's playing a lot of golf. However, I wouldn't want to be stuck behind him on the links while he stares interminably at an old ball perched atop a splintered tee. I do miss watching him in the parking lot, though.

Eight

HEADPHONES

$\mathcal{K}$ate seated Lori, a normally stylish young woman, who looked unusually haggard that day.

"I didn't sleep a wink last night just thinking about this root canal," she confided.

Kate empathized and handed her a Walkman and padded Boise headphones. "You can listen to music instead of the drill," Kate offered.

Lori nervously sighed. "You guys are so nice. Maybe this won't be so bad."

In the early 1900s, "white noise" was introduced as a distraction to put patients at ease. But the irritating hiss was no more relaxing than the grinding of a dental drill. Portable tape players offered a choice of real music. Patient's cranked the volume ever higher when the drill's high-pitched whine began. We had to lift one ear pad to give them instructions: "Open wide" or "Rinse." There was only one drawback. Some folks, especially teens and young adults, would start foot tapping. It's hard to perform delicate work on a moving target.

"We'll do our best to make you comfortable," Kate said, softly placing her hand on Lori's shoulder. "If you need a break, just raise your left hand and I'll have the doctor stop."

"Thanks." Lori smiled crookedly. The Novocain was beginning to take effect.

While the anesthetic performed its magic, Kate arranged instruments and laid several alcohol-gauze pads on her counter.

"You should be good and numb by now, Lori. We'll go ahead and get started," I said.

"OK." Her hands trembled as she positioned the headphones and settled back. The uneventful preparation was soon finished. While I irrigated the tooth with a mild disinfectant, Kate lifted her left ear pad. "Relax, Lori. The worst is over; no more drill." Those once apprehensive eyes softly closed as her body relaxed. She apparently enjoyed Lynyrd Skynyrd's "Sweet Home Alabama," which was turned way up.

It was time to seal the canals with gutta-percha, a gum-like resin. Years ago dentists heated a condenser over an open flame to soften it, creating a tight seal in the canals. Safely maneuvering a red-hot branding iron into someone's moving mouth can be a little dicey. Steady hands are the keys to success.

The Bunsen burner was always lit at the last moment; open flames are not a dentist's best friend. Kate struck the match, which sparked, fizzled then went out. Afraid to press hard on the sulfurous tip, she reluctantly struck again. Once again a puff of unproductive smoke floated up. A little perturbed, I glanced back to see what the delay was. Kate looked a little embarrassed and with renewed determination the third match blazed gloriously.

She fired up the propane and gave me a triumphant look that implied, *See, I did it.* Ever cautious, she placed the burning match on a piece of wet gauze to put it out. But her victory grin suddenly turned south when the gauze burst into flame; it was wet with alcohol!

Kate jumped and her elbow knocked into the blazing burner, but it remained upright. So far the fire was confined to a small piece of cloth on the Formica. "Grab it and throw it into the sink." I gritted through my teeth. As a kid I'd played with fire so much that it didn't seem unusual. Kate thought otherwise, never once having grabbed a fiery brand with her bare hands. Frozen in place, she stared at the flame while Lori's eyes remained closed in detached reverie, ♫*...Lord, I'm comin' home to you...*"♪, totally unaware of the brewing disaster.

"In the sink. Do it, now!" I quietly exclaimed.

Kate blinked and snatched the flaming gauze in her fingers. She aimed for the steel sink but the firebrand fell short, onto a dry paper towel. The liquid spread...well, like wildfire.

Somehow overcoming her fear, Kate grasped the towel and gave a mighty heave. The blaze traced a fiery arc over the sink and landed past it, hard by the wall. During its short flight, the breeze had further fanned the flames.

Who knew that wallpaper would burn so readily?

As the conflagration licked up the operatory wall, I conjured visions of my new office ignominiously disappearing into the shrouds of hell. With as much discretion as I could muster, I jumped up and pitched the bonfire into the sink, filled a green mixing bowl, and splashed water on the wall; a handy lesson I'd learned when Oleander Jacob's hair caught on fire.

With pyrotechnic disaster narrowly averted, I glanced at Kate and managed a weak smile, too relieved to be angry. We breathed a collective sigh of relief as I sat back down on my stool. But Lori's nostrils were flaring like a sniffing bloodhound. Her eyes fluttered open while she pulled away one of the cushioned earpieces. The music was so loud that she yelled, "Is something burning?"

"No, Lori." I affected a calmness I didn't feel. "Everything's just fine. We're simply getting ready for the final phase." Lame. Satisfied, she went back to her music ♫*...Oh, sweet home...*♪ and drifted off while we finished the root canal without further incident.

Upon leaving, she commented on how much she enjoyed using the tape player. "You and Kate make a great team, Dr. James."

Sure—a team of firefighters.

"Thanks so much. And you're a terrific patient." What else could I say?

Nine

THE MOVE

*K*ate and I purchased our first home in Pyleton, a small community about an hour from DC. A few miles upstream is the only working ferry on the Potomac watershed. The drab, battle-gray boat carried fifteen average-sized cars.

Right after we moved to Pyleton, two enormous gravel trucks approached from the Virginia side. The ferry captain scratched his beer belly and spit tobacco juice, then decided: "Load 'em both." The *Stonewall* chugged away from the ramp and slid straight under, swamped just offshore. Waves gently lapped while the truck's back tires walked on water.

The *Pyleton News*, a four-page tabloid featured a grainy front-page photo of a crane unloading the waterlogged trucks. The *Stonewall* floated to the surface and was soon back in business—with a new helmsman.

Water consumption stole most *News* headlines during the dry summer months. If a public well fell below critical, the paper would announce: "Anyone caught watering their lawn will be fined $50," with a fine print concession: "Payable in two easy installments."

"Anyone washing a car must replenish the water." How?

One good ole boy, tired of farming, built a self-service car wash on Main Street. Forced to remain idle for half the summer, it soon failed. The ugly block structure stood empty for years as a reminder to keep your garden hose stowed.

The *News* featured myriad community activities: Boy Scouts, Girl Scouts, Odd Fellows, Lions Club, church bazaars, and the vaunted Pyleton Piranha Swim Team. I had to wonder where they got water for the pool.

In Floyd's Barbershop, an old redbrick building at the four-way stop, you could catch up on *Field & Stream, Guns & Gardens,* and rumors. Floyd quickly removed any *People* magazines left behind.

The Odd Fellows Hall was upstairs next to a dental office; both shared a street-level door. The smell of hair tonics, kitchen grease, and dental clove wafted along Main Street. Dr. Patel practiced only two days a week while I sublet his office and equipment on Thursdays. On Wednesdays he rented to Dr. Heel, a podiatrist!

Right after Kate and I wed, Dr. Patel blindsided me by packing up and leaving town. Kate notified my patients that they'd have to drive twenty miles to Rockville; most of them looked for a closer dentist. Kate began the search for a house big enough to accommodate an office.

Jim, a neighbor from Brooklyn, didn't want us to move. "What's wrong wit' us?"

"Nuthin'. I just can't put a dental office in my townhouse and—"

"You'se make me sick. I taught we was friends."

The For Sale sign in our front lawn disappeared a couple of times. Maybe it wasn't Jim—after all, he was a cop—but the culprit was never discovered.

Jim, a diehard Giants fan, loathed the Redskins. At a time when Joe Gibb's team was winning big, Jim gloated when Joe Theisman's leg was accidentally snapped by Lawrence Taylor of the Giants. Jim kept a videotape of it.

Jim poked fun at my subtle southern accent, just like my "Joisey" friends did. He accused anyone with a "hick accent" of bigotry, which was ironic because he patrolled DC's inner city with a big German Shepherd that he named Sambo, who was actually quite cuddly—Sambo, not Jim.

"Sooo…Jim. How do you get Sambo to act?"

With an evil smirk he recited, "A-t-t-a-c-k."

Jim and Wanda's townhouse was never vandalized. They liked to party-hearty, filling their house with rowdy revelers. But few became as inebriated as host and hostess.

We'd purchased our place from George, who walked to the party from his new home in Pyleton. Jim shouted. "Hey Georgie boy. Whadda ya doin'? Slumming it?"

George would grin. "Only tonight."

George and his wife, Ann, were very active in their diocese and local charities, very compassionate folks. And George had a great sense of humor. They were our bowling partners for several years.

While leaning against a kitchen counter, George and I talked about my furnace problems. "The coil does burn out; try replacing it. Call me if that doesn't work." George tipped his Solo cup, found it empty, and headed toward the keg. "You want another one, Carroll?"

"Nah. I'm fine. Maybe later."

While chatting with another neighbor, I remembered my drippy sink and asked of no one in particular, "I wonder where George went off to?"

Jim's wife leaned into me. "Oh, heesh schlepped ou' back ta water the bushes." I turned away toward the living room.

"Thanks, Wanda."

Ann saw me standing alone in a corner. "Have you seen my adolescent husband, Carroll?" She looked a bit concerned. George had imbibed more than his usual that night.

"I'll look around, Ann. I heard he might be out back."

"Thanks. He's probably OK, but just to be sure…."

Jim's postage-stamp backyard bordered the high school athletic fields. Without the game lights on, it was quite dark. Stepping boldly into the blackness of a crisp, cool evening, I saw that Sambo's cage was open. *That was odd.*

I further focused and saw two legs splayed across the grass. Sambo straddled them, his front paws firmly planted on his victim's chest. His tail wasn't wagging and his face was hung only inches from George's face.

Fairly inebriated, George had stumbled against the unlatched gate and landed halfway inside the cage. Sambo had probably had George trapped like this since he came outside. His distinct, gravelly voice floated plaintively in the darkness. "Help me. Please, for God's sake." Sambo growled gutturally.

Sambo never acknowledged me. I didn't even try to coax him off, knowing only one command: "A-t-t-a-c-k." That wouldn't help much.

"I'll get Jim straight away. Now don't you go anywhere." I laughed and ran inside through the dense throng of revelers. Jim was on the far side of the living room, tottering while hanging on to the couch.

"Hey, Jim! Sambo's got George trapped out back."

"Wha'? Can't hear you'se."

"Sambo's pinned George to the ground," I yelled. "Get out there."

As Jim stumbled into the backyard a big grin spread across his flushed face. "What'll ya give me ta get him off, George?"

"That's not funny you dumb son of a bitch." George was in no mood to negotiate. Sambo growled louder and further tensed.

"I'd keep your voice down Georgie boy." Jim feigned leaving. "Sambo don't like yellin'."

George softly pleaded. "I'll buy ya a beer or two. Just git 'em off me."

"Fair enough. But I'll be specting those beers." Jim got serious. "Sambo! Release!" The powerful shepherd sat down and nuzzled Jim's hand.

Well, that was easy. I felt stupid.

George stood up, zipped up, and then more or less walked inside to find Ann. A little embarrassed, he said to her, "Let's go home."

Kate found an affordable home just outside of town. Our contract was contingent on selling our townhouse. Jim gave us grief.

"Movin' to the fancy neighborhood?"

"It's only four blocks away; and it's not fancy."

"Whatever," he grumbled.

Months passed without a nibble on our place. I suspected Jim might've chased off a prospective buyer or two; he and Sambo were hanging out in front more than usual.

"Ya know, Carroll, a storm blew down our row before it was finished." He put his foot on the For Sale sign. "Hard to sell a place been knocked over by a little wind."

I stared up at the water tower. It hovered dark and menacing as a strong gust kicked up. *Maybe I'll lower the asking price.*

Our ninety day contract had just expired when fate interceded. A teenager sped into town, missed the tight turn, and clobbered the old house, which now had to be repaired. Then a tractor trailer jackknifed into it. It was never meant to be ours. Kate continued to scan the real estate listings.

We returned home from church on a fine Sunday afternoon and plopped down on the couch, secretly hoping the other would slap a couple of sandwiches together.

"You hungry?"

"Nah."

"Yeah, me neither," she smiled while shaking out the Sunday paper. "Let's drive over after we eat and look at a place in Gloyd." That was my cue to make lunch.

"Sure," I agreed while making two PB&Js, my specialty.

The beautiful, rolling five acres was only fifteen minutes away. Two horses and a John Deere farm tractor conveyed with the sale. Having grown up with horses, I love everything about them; even the cracked ribs and busted knee I'd gotten along the way. Despite these perks, the house, sheds, and barn weren't finished.

"This is a twenty year project," Kate observed.

"I'm game if you are," I grinned. I do like a challenge.

However, $197,500 was more than we could afford; we underbid by $30,000. After three weeks, Tom the realtor called. "I have a contract. I'll drop it by tonight."

That evening I looked out the kitchen window and saw Tom pause to look for the missing For Sale sign. I opened the door before he knocked. "So, what's the deal?"

"Look at this." He plopped a packet down on the kitchen table. "It's for $137,500." That was not only $43,000 less than the asking price, it was $13,000 less than our offer; the guy was bidding *down*! "I think you should sign," Tom suggested.

"There's something fishy about it," I muttered.

"We need time to think it over," Kate echoed. In the end, we took it, contingent on the sale of our townhouse.

Three months went by and not a bite on our home; Pyleton real estate languished. The seller, Dick, agreed to re-up for another ninety days. Two more months had gone by when our phone rang.

"Carroll, the bank's gonna foreclose." Dick sounded desperate. "But if I sell the farm I can pay off my mortgage and also buy your house." We agreed. The bank was happy, Dick was relieved, and we were ecstatic.

The settlement was attorney chaos with papers flying helter-skelter across the mahogany conference table. "Sign here and initial this box." Thirty years later I still wonder if it was all legal; we must have squatter's rights by now. But the confusion of settlement paled compared to swapping houses on the same day.

In March of 1983, DC's biggest blizzard in years blanketed the area while the next day dawned sunny with a cool breeze; perfect moving conditions. We'd hired a company to move the heavy furniture at an hourly rate. With friends and family helping with the small stuff, we hoped it would go quickly.

The convoy of cars, pickups, and moving van soon pulled onto the gravel lane of our new home. "Pull around back," I shouted to the van's driver.

"The ground's awfully soggy," he grunted.

"Don't worry about it, as long as you can make it to the back door."

He turned the corner and stopped dead. Halfway Dick, the half builder of our new home, had blocked the door with his six-wheel pickup. But my movers were on the clock, and I was almost broke after unforeseen settlement costs. I rushed into the house. "Hey, Dick. Move your truck out of the way!"

He looked up from the open refrigerator door. "We'll be done in an hour or so." That meant much later in the day.

Frustrated, I admonished, "Look; do you want to pay these guys to stand around?"

He saw my point. "Kids, grab the lamps and ashtrays." His wife quickly threw condiments into a Playmate cooler.

I took a deep breath. "Dick, if you pull your truck closer to the door the van can get around to the glass slider." While the trucks jockeyed, I paused to enjoy the magnificent view of rolling farmland. *It'll all work out.*

To make room for our stuff, Dick soon cleared the living room except for his Harley-Davidson, which I'd agreed he could get later. We unloaded through the sliding glass door while Dick vacated out the kitchen door. Toting light-weight boxes, his kids ran into walls and tripped over lamp cords. Chaos reigned. A few of our boxes went full circuit. We had to later fetch them from Dick's house, our old Pyleton home.

That reminded me of our first trip to the Pyleton grocery store. My two kids from a first marriage, Tara and Russell, came to live with us and helped stock our townhome from scratch, filling three grocery carts to overflowing with spices, cereals, and canned goods along with detergents, toiletries, and light bulbs.

The rain was blowing sideways when we came out of the store. I ran to get our beat-up Pinto wagon and turned the wipers up full blast. I hit the curb then stopped while Kate and the kids made a dash for it with bags of groceries.

"C'mon guys. Get it all in before it gets soaked." After several trips through the pouring rain, they had the car packed. "Man that's a lot of stuff," I muttered.

"You should see the bill, Carroll. Then again, maybe you shouldn't."

I backed up to our townhouse and opened the hatch. "One more time, guys. Let's see how fast we can do this." Tara had to be prodded, but Russell's lanky legs seemed to quickly skirt between the raindrops. The storm door slammed shut as Tara scooted through with the last soggy brown bag.

The kids made themselves scarce while I emptied the myriad goods onto kitchen counters while Kate decided where it all would go. After putting cleansers under the sink, she stood up to straighten her back. "What's all that stuff, Carroll?"

"What stuff?"

She pointed to a pile on the counter. "That can of curry and the egg noodles. And I thought you didn't like anchovies. I know I don't."

"I hate anchovies and curry. I thought you picked 'em up."

"Well, I didn't."

We stared at each other and grinned. In the confusion we'd unloaded not only our carts, but also someone else's. It was back to the store where Mrs. Shelby knew exactly whose food it was.

But when we moved to Gloyd, it wasn't raining. The waterbed was a chore to assemble. After wrestling with its heavy frame, I snaked a garden hose through a window and hooked it up. Soon there was a shallow layer of water in the bladder. *This is gonna take a while.* I left to do other things.

Kate vacuumed and scrubbed the rooms we'd be using; the Harley grease spot was a lost cause. We camouflaged it with an air hockey table that Santa later brought. Kate arranged our eclectic family room furniture, which we later moved again. I piled plates, pans, glasses, and cutlery on the counter. She decided where they went—and later moved them again. I still can't find anything.

Running water waits for no man.

"Dad! Come quick!" Russell sounded frantic.

"Hurry up," Tara echoed.

"Where are you two?"

"In your bedroom." I had to stop and think where that was. Bounding down the hallway, I pulled up short at the doorway. The bladder was bloated far above the waterbed's frame, thinned almost to the point of exploding. It looked like The Blob.

So what did I do? I dug out the camera. It's a great picture.

After snapping a few shots, I disconnected the hose but forgot to turn the faucet off; water sprayed our dressers, end tables, ceiling, unfinished drywall, and the cigarette-burned carpet. It was a good time to break for lunch.

Sitting around with friends and family, we had a few laughs. The beers helped. And then it was time for them to say good-bye. Although exhausted, Kate and I worked for several more hours while Tara and Russell slipped away to explore the farm and pet the horses.

Russell came in, smelling of manure. "What's for supper?"

"We'll go out for pizza, buddy. Tell your sister we'll go in about a half hour."

"Okay, Dad. But I'm starved."

I sighed and looked to Kate, who was on the couch with her eyes closed, feigning sleep. "I'll tell you what, pal. By the time you round up Tara we'll be ready."

He smiled and ran off. Weary, I nodded off while the sun sank toward the horizon. Somewhere in my brain fog, I heard a commotion. "What's up?"

"Dad!" Russell yelled from the void. "Come quick."

I stretched and rolled over while Kate barely stirred.

"C'mon, Dad. Get up."

Maybe Tara had an accident. Did she fall out of the hayloft? "Is your sister OK?"

"She's out front watching it."

"Watching what?" Kate woke up looking anxious.

"C'mon!"

Tara, sitting on the front stoop, pointed across Stabletown Road to a field that was ablaze and spreading. I imagined fire jumping the narrow country road and raging up our hill to burn down our new home. What to do? Grab the camera, of course. It's what I always do—another great picture.

"Did you call the fire department?" I asked Kate after framing the shot.

"Nope. Our phones aren't hooked up yet." She ran next door as the wail of fire engines insulted the quiet country evening. The neighbor had already called.

Apparently a firefighter had started a controlled burn to clear a site for his new house. After a few too many beers with his friends, they stopped tending the fire. When it blazed out of control, he radioed for help.

Tara and Russell stayed up late while Kate and I finally fell into our distended waterbed, exhausted and not caring what they did. Tomorrow was another day.

A dramatic eight by ten photo of the brush fire hangs in my waiting room but not a picture of the stressed bladder, which began to leak after a few nights. Waking up in a puddle of water got old, and we soon graduated to a real bed. Gloyd was already home.

A few years later, our good friend George was killed in a tragic road rage incident. He was one of two innocent commuters who died on the way to work, along with one of the perpetrators. The other is still behind bars in a case that became nationally infamous. But the new awareness didn't come in time for George and his family. He and Ann were deeply in love. She never remarried.

George is sorely missed by all whose lives he touched.

Ten

NATALIA

An attractive bleached-blond doll answered our ad for a certified assistant. Although not certified, she was personable, enthusiastic, and eager to learn; I hired her on the spot.

"Kate, I think we've found a good one."

Natalia (her pretty name fit her dainty physique) picked up four-handed dentistry faster than Kate had. However, she fumbled radiographs, as if nervous about radiation. But I wasn't fooled—the girl wasn't afraid of much—and overlooked this because she was great at everything else. I took most of the X-rays.

When Kate was on maternity leave and later when she stayed home with baby Joel, Natalia easily doubled as receptionist/assistant. She was more than capable at juggling her duties. But like the X-rays, she had one flaw at reception: telephone etiquette, which even those high-tech phones couldn't improve.

"I don't have a clue...maybe...insurance isn't my thing. Listen, do you want an appointment or not? Look, I'm helping him right now. I'll check with Kate when I'm not busy."

Click!

However, that harsh attitude came in handy when rude or uncooperative patients called. They'd meet their match in our cute, deceptively petite receptionist; a delicate doily she was not.

"No, he's busy…Yeah, I'll tell him…Well how should I know?" Click.

"Uh…that wasn't a patient, was it Natalia?"

"Nah, just some sales guy." *Well, that's OK then.*

She was very calming in the operatory and could be quite pleasant on the phone with folks she knew. But without warning, Ms. Jekyll would turn into Dr. Hyde, especially if a patient canceled at the last minute or called to say he was running late.

"Great! I'll just tell Doc he's gotta stand around cause of you."

Disagreeable or argumentative patients wound up with the worst appointment times: early morning, late afternoon, or lunchtime. Dr. Hyde was merciless.

But the good Ms. Jekyll miraculously reappeared—perky, pleasant, and helpful—if she liked you. If you were unknown, Natalia would be polite but indifferent. The telephone was not her thing, except when chatting with her friends.

"It's the best new spa in town," she'd whisper.

"Natalia, I'm ready to take the impression," I might sing out.

"I'm on the business line just now. I'll be right there," she'd falsely promise. "Gotta go. Tonight? Sure. How 'bout eight?"

"Natalia!"

"I said I'm coming!" She'd shout back. "See you later, Franie."

Getting her skinny butt chairside was especially frustrating if I was treating someone on the out-of-favor-with-Natalie list. I suspect that she *initiated* such important calls at those times.

Her forte would always be assisting, preferring the fast pace that develops during a busy day. If we had to squeeze in an emergency patient, she'd kick into high gear. And she was adept at handling fire during those intense root canals; a real plus!

Natalia complemented her striking looks with meticulous care. Kate said she frequently dyed her hair, but I couldn't tell. And fashionable clothes were a must. She never wore the same outfit twice, which I also learned from Kate.

Natalia never put makeup on in the office. She'd rather arrive late for work than be "unprepared." Actually, she was routinely late. But she always managed to get the office up and running on time so I also overlooked that.

She was all feminine mystique, except at mealtime. Packing an enormous bag lunch (much larger than mine and I'm not small), she ate like a mountain logger.

On one gorgeous day when Kate stopped by, I took everyone out to lunch. While dining on the patio, I discreetly watched Natalia wolf down a humongous sub with the intensity of a Rottweiler. I unwittingly blurted, "So…Natalia. How do you manage to stay so thin?"

Kate glared and hit my arm. Natalia's grinding slowed to a halt. A puzzled look swept across her face. Her jaw clenched and I panicked. *Uh oh. I'm in trouble now…big time.* My eyes darted every which way, looking for an escape route.

A large bolus of food indelicately ballooned her left cheek as she calmly replied. "This is my only meal of the day." She shrugged her delicate shoulders and immediately returned to the task at hand, devouring her fully loaded Italian sub. I breathed a sigh of relief.

Natalia loved to read soap opera tabloids. Seated at the front desk with her head cradled in one hand, her light blue eyes would scan a digest's shiny pages. When I tried to steal a glance, she'd sense my presence and judiciously slide it under a stack of insurance forms. I'd sometimes ask, "Why hasn't Ms. Smith's insurance been submitted?" or "Have you copied that chart yet?" She had several patent answers:

"You (meaning me) scribbled it illegibly." Admittedly, that was not uncommon.

"That idiot patient didn't give me all the necessary information." It happens, even with non-idiots.

"You didn't fill everything out." Again, it was my fault.

Somehow folks on her A-list had complete, perfectly legible charts. When I would turn to walk away, the digest would slowly emerge from the pile, as if pulled by some invisible force, and magically reappear by the time I turned the corner.

While Natalia went out to run an errand one day, curiosity got the better of me; I skimmed through one of the stories. Here's the gist:

Lance had sired Tiffany's baby, suggesting that Steele was not the father. Readers had to wait to find out if Kelli, thrown into a jealous rage, would abscond with Lance's frozen assets from the sperm bank, accidentally switched with Steel's, a fact that wouldn't be revealed until next season. So, is Steel actually the real father? Stay tuned!

Any attempt to remove her soap opera road map meant risking a hand.

Natalia spent what I thought was an inordinate amount of time and effort fussing over her fingernails. My rule was to answer the phone by three rings. If it struck six bells, I knew she was probably busy painting and didn't want them smudged.

Although our instruments had always been autoclaved, we seldom wore gloves in the mid-70s; vigorous hand washing was the standard of care. Concerned with cleanliness, I insisted on no extraneous rings, watches, bracelets, or tinted fingernails. Chipped polish is unavoidable after numerous scrubbings and even though clean, it might not look so to a patient.

Natalia dutifully removed her rings and bracelets (she didn't wear a watch since she was not concerned with being late), but stubbornly disregarded my nail polish directive. I tried to compromise. "Natalia, you can use clear but that bright pink is too much."

Narrowing her eyes with fixed determination, she declared, "You cannot *possibly* expect me to go out in public like this!" She'd deftly blame me if she was not perfectly attired for her evening date. How do you argue with that? But I tried to, stammering something about the rules. She stared at me with those deceptively soft baby blues, which now seemed to harbor an ominous hint of fire red.

I averted my eyes from her laser glare and changed the subject. "I once cracked a rib, playing golf of all things. Have you ever broken anything, Natalia?"

"A nail," she replied through pursed lips before returning to her emery board sculpting.

The battle over fingernail paint would be an uphill one that I'd never win. And her slender, graceful fingers presented quite nicely due to her fastidiousness. I decided it was a nonissue. Or maybe I'm just a wimp.

All of this might imply that Natalia was a slacker, wasting time doing her fingernails, reading soaps, primping, and chatting on the phone with friends. However, when we were overly busy, she'd work like a banshee. But if our schedule was light, she didn't pretend to work when there was nothing to do. I silently admired her honesty in this. She was loyal and dedicated, which counted for a lot.

Natalia was comfortably settled into her double-duty routine when I hired an associate dentist. Kate wasn't quite ready to return to work, and the dentist needed space immediately. Just out of school, Dr. Suliman Lee was miserable in her first job and hated her old boss. To help out, I funneled her a few patients, but not many.

The added burden on Natalia wasn't fair. Dr. Lee's English was marginal, and she advertised exclusively in the local Korean newspaper. All of her patients spoke Korean, most of them only Korean.

Natalia spoke only English. "What! I can't understand you," she'd yell into the phone. "Why don't you call back when Dr. Lee's here? Oh, I give up." *Click.* "Hey, Dr. C. I can't take this crap. Get Sun-what's-her-name to make her own appointments."

Crap was the only cuss word I ever heard Natalia utter, and she used it sparingly, only when dealing with Dr. Lee.

I would try to defuse the situation with humor. "I've got an idea, Natalia. Why don't you take night classes in Korean?"

Her only answer was that icy stare.

Dr. Lee installed another phone line, which Natalia absolutely refused to answer. Helping a struggling associate wasn't in her job description, and, frankly, I'd already dumped a lot on her. Dr. Lee struggled along for a year or so until she found a full-time job across town. Like with Dr. Friedan, private practice wasn't for her.

Natalia was happy.

In late March, Natalia, obsessed with sun and sand, would get in shape for the beach. And not with a rigorous exercise program; I can't picture her breaking a sweat on a treadmill. And weights were out; she might fracture a nail.

To get in shape, Natalia made regular trips to the Tan N Glow. She wouldn't think of showing up at Dewey Beach with a sickly pallor. That's no way to show off a new bikini. Before Memorial Day, her alabaster skin had turned deep copper brown.

The first time I noticed, I asked, "Natalia, are you using iodine or something?" She answered with that piercing, slit-eyed glare. How could I even suggest that she'd stoop to crummy lotions!

Some folks might look for the blooming of snow crocuses to herald spring. For me, when Natalia took her first trip to the House of Tan, I knew summer was just around the corner.

After her first beach weekend, our schedule would subtly alter. As the days grew longer, our Friday workday became shorter. When she controlled the phones, not a single soul was booked on Friday afternoons. And as spring flowed into summer, morning appointments became scarce. We might wrap up as early as 10 A.M.

Whenever the last patient left, she was out the door, roaring away in her sporty compact to avoid weekend traffic. "See ya' Monday, Dr. C." I'd hear from a blur running down the hallway.

When July rolled around, she wore a lab coat for our "rigorous" two-hour morning. She wore her beach garb—shorts and a halter-top—under the coat. I feared that it might someday slip off her petite frame, but never said anything. Again, I'm a wimp. And she did keep it carefully wrapped. Thankfully, a wardrobe malfunction never happened.

For most folks, short cool days are the first signs of fall; mums bloom, birds wing their way south, and trees burst forth in glorious colors. But my autumn barometer was Friday's patient load, which would slowly lengthen. By late fall, Natalia would arrive for work, dressed normally and still a little late.

She eventually moved to the shore but does stop by our house for a friendly visit when in town. Kate once asked how she likes her new boss in Delaware.

"Oh, I like him a lot." With a bright smile and twinkling eyes, she added, "He's a lot like you; doesn't get in my way!" The tanning salon lost a regular customer, and I lost a trusted and valued assistant.

But not a friend.

Eleven

DOGGONE IT

Our new Gloyd farmette needed a dog. Kate had small dogs as a kid; I liked big ones. "I don't want some little yappy thing."

She agreed to one large enough to complement our horses and went to the pound with her sister, Annette. They were drawn to one in particular.

"I love this mutt," Annette squealed.

"Me too," echoed Kate. "But I'll have to show Carroll first."

Later that day, I agreed to stop by the pound on the way home from work the following day. "We'll take the truck. Even if I like him, I won't want him in my sporty BMW."

Kate, back at work part time, got more excited toward the end of the day and faked interest in what the last patient was saying, which was a lot of nothing. As soon as "gabby" was out the door—long after Natalia who, at this point, was still working for us—Kate grabbed her purse.

"Let's go." Work had been particularly vexing, and I sported a huge headache that unmercifully pounded as we approached the county pound.

The drab cinderblock building resembled a prison. Inside its stark lobby, a beefy receptionist sat behind a gray metal desk.

She was clad in dirty work boots, a faded flannel shirt, and grimy overalls. Her dirty-blond pigtails curled below her ruddy cheeks; pale-blue eyes stared hard, as if daring us to cross her. Attila the Hun's sister.

Although we were the only folks in the small lobby, she shouted, "Next!" which echoed painfully in my skull. After robotically firing a barrage of questions, she buzzed us into cell block "C."

"Be sure to follow the rules and behave yourselves."

"Does she expect us to break the dogs out of jail?" I whispered to Kate while rubbing my temples.

"Shhh, Carroll," she quietly admonished and then smiled at the receptionist, who didn't smile back.

After passing through a steel door with a wire-mesh bulletproof window, we entered Dante's *Inferno*; the sound of meowing, hissing, barking, and growling emanated from deep within. Endless rows of cages were piled one atop another. "They're kinda small."

"Those are for cats," Kate patiently explained. With the terrible acoustics in the building, it was hard to hear her over the cacophony of noise. Then I noticed the pungent stench; the smell of feces, urine, and festering wounds were poorly disguised by the Lysol and Clorox the workers had added to the odiferous mix. *So this is purgatory.*

"Carroll, you OK?" Kate knew I'd had a hard day.

"It's nothing." I probably looked shell-shocked.

"We can always come back tomorrow; your call."

"No. Let's just get it over with." Seemed like now would be better than coming back. I was wrong.

We worked our way down narrow aisles of screeching felines with arched Halloween backs and trudged onward to *The Dungeon of Damned Dogs.* Many snarled as if they wanted nothing less than to take a chunk out of my leg. While winding through the maze of pens, I daydreamed about my college summers when I worked as a mailman and dogs just waited to take a turn at me.

I was thinking of the one that actually attacked me when Kate grabbed my hand. I jumped.

She squealed, "He's down here at the far end." The "far" end; one more gauntlet to run.

The imprisoned mutt was lanky and reddish, a mix of Irish setter and maybe forty other breeds—all very large. In her excitement, Kate yanked me close to the chain link door. I rubbed my whiplashed neck as the beast suddenly leapt at me and planted his front paws on the wire gate, which ominously bowed outward. Surprised, I stumbled a half step back.

Standing on his hind legs, the creature looked me in the eyes and furiously panted. His breath was incredibly bad, his tongue the longest I'd ever seen; he drooled a river. Scraggly hairs of indiscriminate colors protruded from a Matterhorn lump atop his head.

It was one of the mangiest, smelliest, ugliest inmates in the whole place—one only a mother could love. Kate was beaming "That's him."

Gathering what little composure I could muster, I focused on the bio posted on his cage; Rusty. It was an appropriate name for a rogue, reddish animal. Under "Distinguishing Characteristics" the four by six card proclaimed, "loose stools."

Great! Kate and Annette picked out an eighty-five pound dog with diarrhea.

Desperate for relief from the racket, I whimpered, "Let's adopt him and go home." Deliriously happy, Kate cradled my head in both her hands and planted a big kiss on my forehead. Whether it was for me or the mutt, it didn't really matter. With her loving touch, my headache receded.

We kept the name Rusty. He had a friendly disposition, and the family quickly grew to love him—even me, after his runs abated. He enjoyed following us on horseback rides through the woods across the way, often accompanied by an enormous yellow lab named Josh.

Our introduction to Josh—before we got Rusty—was a bit rocky. I'd inadvertently left the back door ajar one night shortly after we moved in to our new Gloyd home. The next morning, Kate climbed bleary-eyed from bed and shuffled down the hall to fire up the coffee maker. I was still lying in the leaky waterbed when I heard a blood-curdling scream.

"Carroll. Come quick!"

Dashing from the bedroom, I found my trembling wife plastered against the kitchen wall, pointing to a humongous dirty-white beast beside the coffee table. His hefty head was cocked to one side with ears forward and tail furiously wagging; it soon cleared the coffee table of magazines, coasters, and pretty much everything.

To me, he didn't look threatening; more amused at all the commotion. "Come 'ere boy." I coaxed him outside with a morsel of leftover beef, which he downed in one gulp. We instantly became good friends.

Although Josh technically belonged to our neighbor Dan he freely wandered the Gloyd countryside. Seeing us astride our mounts, he'd fall in line behind the last horse; sometimes he got a little too close. On more than one occasion, a fresh load of processed grass would plop onto Josh's head, but he didn't seem to mind. Rusty played it safe, constantly running hither and yon, out of sight but nearby, somewhere in the brush.

Rusty's dog bowl periodically disappeared. "It might be those strong winds that roar up our hillside," I suggested. I bought a weighted one, which soon vanished. The same with a third bowl. We were totally baffled.

One day, while gazing out the bedroom window, Kate saw Josh slowly saunter down the driveway with a brand new dog dish clamped in his steel jaws. She followed him to the church rectory across Stabletown Road. His undulating hips disappeared around the corner. Kate knocked on the front door and the pastor's wife opened it a crack.

"Yes?"

"I'm Kate from across the street. Do you have any bowls that aren't yours?"

She smiled and stepped outside. "Lordy, honey, come look under my deck." There was a treasure trove of stolen goods: kids toys, doggy dinnerware, and ladies undergarments torn from numerous clotheslines. Josh was a kleptomaniac. For some unknown reason, he routinely deposited his stolen goods under the pastor's deck. Was it Josh's tithe?

Kate retrieved a few familiar items. "Carroll, look at all these bowls. How are we going to keep Josh from stealing them again?"

"I'll think of something." I drilled a heavy-duty hook into a bowl and clipped it to a chain that I nailed to our deck. It still hangs there today, rusted, weather-beaten, and now unused.

On the rural farmette that I grew up on, my father laid down strict rules about pets. "They belong outdoors. I never want to see a dog, cat, or anything else inside." When I was about eight, I broke that rule by bringing my Shetland Pony, Smokey, through the screened porch and into the kitchen. My mother looked up and screamed. My father came running, and I received a good tanning. But I think Smokey enjoyed exploring the house.

Kate grew up in suburbia with a fish tank, two small dogs, and a squirrel monkey; all had the run of the house—except the fish.

This led to the inevitable clash of wills. I won the first round. "Rusty stays outdoors." Quite possibly his "loose stools" strengthened my argument. There was never any question about the horses. I post mounted a large dinner bell to summon Rusty, who roamed free like Josh, the same way Dad had called me and Lee home. It took a while for Rusty to learn about the bell, but he finally got it after one traumatic episode.

Shortly after we sprang him from doggy detention, a driving thunderstorm blew through the upper county. Flashes of lightning crackled ever closer, lighting up the sky. Solid sheets of rain pelted the house. Rusty pressed his sad mug against the glass door; he was drenched. With limp ears, he forlornly gazed into our warm, dry family room.

"Please let him in," Kate pleaded. "Just until it's over."

"Rules are rules. He'll be perfectly fine in that doghouse I built him." *Stupid dog, go into your doghouse.* I closed the drapes. "It's the natural order of things. He'll live."

The following morning dawned bright, the air scrubbed clean by the rain.

"Rusty's missing," Kate frantically yelled. I scoured the fields on foot while Kate drove around. He was nowhere to be found. Feeling unloved, Rusty had taken his chances against the blinding rain. Kate was furious with me. Now *I* was in the doghouse.

Three days later, the Pyleton woman who'd originally given him up to the pound (probably the loose stools) contacted our vet. Rusty had somehow made it cross-country to her place. She'd locked him in the garage and called her vet, the same one we used. "Rusty's safe and sound," the vet announced over my office phone.

"Great. We'll run by after work." I was elated. Kate was making life miserable for me.

Toward the end of the day, the lady called back. "My husband got home, hit the garage door opener, and Rusty escaped."

Kate blamed me.

The next few days around the James's household were gloomy. Kate barely spoke to me—probably for the best. I checked the shelters daily, then twice daily. Receptionists began to recognize my voice and got irritated. The Hun at the county pound sounded especially scary. "Look, stop calling; you're more trouble than the animals." *Click.*

I was desperate when a housewife just down the road called.

"This is Teresa, of Teresa's Treasures. I picked up a stray. Might be yours." She'd seen my "Missing" poster in the country store. At the end of his fifteen-mile round-trip trek, Rusty had missed us by only half a mile.

Kate went with me to pick him up. When Rusty, health and happy, saw us, his tail wagged as if we were long lost friends. His tag was missing, lost somewhere between Gloyd and Pyleton. Back home, he hopped from the car and licked my hand. Dogs are the most forgiving animals in the world; a lesson people might take to heart.

From that time on, he was allowed inside on select occasions and never, *ever* left outside in a thunderstorm. Kate continued to chip away at my armor until he eventually slept inside the house. Sometimes in our bedroom! Miracles do happen. Or maybe penance is forever. The doghouse rotted away.

"We live on a farm and need a cat." I thought now was a good time to broach the subject of a mouser.

"I hate cats! They scare me." Kate was definite.

When a large family of mice moved into the kitchen, Kate freaked and that weekend we had two newly weaned kittens. Named after Kate's favorite TV characters, Lucy and Ethel were sisters. I brought them inside and sat them on the kitchen hearth; I'd come a long way. Rusty drooled, like they were appetizers. But he soon realized they were also family and cuddled with them in front of the fire.

Many years later, Lucy disappeared on the very same day Lucille Ball passed away. Eerie.

Twelve

My brother and I were raised in the "ruburbs": rolling farmland beyond DC's suburban sprawl. Although lower middle class, we never lacked life's necessities. As a self-made man with little education, my dad did OK selling orthopedic shoe inserts; he'd been quite an entrepreneur in his day. However, the plight of Mom and her family was quite different.

Every summer my parents loaded our big Buick gas-guzzler and headed south to Mom's homestead, a small clapboard farmhouse in the impoverished backwoods of southwestern Virginia. With the car packed for the entire summer, Lee and I were crammed into the backseat with dry goods for Grandma.

It took us forever to get to Nealy Ridge, slowed to a crawl by innumerable one-horse towns with four-way stops. Lee and I fought every mile of the two-day trek up the Shenandoah Valley. When Dad got fed up with us, his arm would swing back; he didn't care who he hit, as long as he made contact with flesh. The drive can now be done in air-conditioned comfort in about seven hours on I-81.

Once in Dickenson County (the least populated county in Virginia, then and now) Dad would cautiously maneuver his bulky sedan up treacherous one-lane dirt roads that coursed precipitately along craggy cliffs. My city-boy father got more nervous as we climbed ever higher into a time warp of log cabins and log barns, outhouses, draw wells—seldom a pump—and split-rail snake fences that vaguely defined parched, rocky hayfields. A one-room schoolhouse was reminiscent of the 1800s rather than the prosperous 1950s.

For the most part, mountain folk didn't have cash-money jobs. As subsistence farmers, they ate the produce they grew, the livestock they raised, and the game they hunted. Grandpa did earn a little hard currency by selling raw timber from his land or the adjoining wilds; it was hard to tell where one began and the other ended.

With a much longer drive from Detroit, Aunt Aida and her boys, Bart and David, joined us on those down-home summers. Clyde rounded out us five cousins. Clyde's dad—Uncle Joel—no longer resided in the mountains although he remained in the South, just off the two-lane pike that meandered through the beautiful Valley.

Our grandparents scratched out a hard life of humble poverty in much the same way as their parents and their parents before them had. Mom and Aunt Aida helped work the farm while we boys hiked the rugged hills and wandered the hollers, entertained by nature's playground. The time away from my comfortable suburban home was an opportunity to experience America's pioneering spirit as a living laboratory. And, by degrees, I became a participant as much as an observer.

As a young kid I was never afraid to roam those steep hills and low valleys where folks always made you feel at home. However, a respectful fear of big cats, black bears, and poisonous snakes was definitely in order. People who were ostensibly strangers, although they always seemed to know exactly who I was, on more than one occasion took me in when I was lost, which happened all too often, and fed me before making sure I made my way home. The degenerate hillbillies of *Deliverance* were Hollywood, not real life.

Those folks never complained about not wearing the latest fashion or having a new car; many would never own an automobile and clothes were often patched hand-me-downs. But they were generous, almost to a fault—salt of the earth. I acquired a healthy respect for a work ethic all too often lacking today. It sounds like a cliché, but I know few people who work as hard for as little as my grandparents did. But I risk idealization; like everyone, they did have their share of faults and shortcomings.

Living in the days of yore was physically demanding, even for resilient young bucks like my cousins and me. Not much changed from year to year; we simply grew taller and the old folks older. But lots of fun was had, which often—maybe too often—involved a hefty dose of juvenile mischief.

And as much as I loved those summers, I grew to realize that life on Nealy Ridge was primitive, tough, and full of hard lessons never dreamed of by my contemporaries. At summer's end, we piled into our gas-guzzling "time machine" and journeyed back to the 20th century with all its modern conveniences.

Out of familial respect, I recreated the honest labors of my ancestors on our small farmette in Gloyd. Feeding the livestock, tending the fields, and chopping firewood have been therapeutic for me. Whenever my kids, Tara, Russell, and Joel complained that they were "bored," I'd put them to work. They've carried more firewood, limed more fields, and mucked more stalls than they would've liked. I've tried to instill in them an appreciation for the hard work needed to survive throughout much of the world. At the same time, whenever I got sick—or lazy—we never went cold in the winter. The central heat kicked in.

When I was told in tenth grade that dentists "have it made," I thought of my Appalachian relatives who decidedly *did not* have it made. I reflected on the disparity of their life struggle with that of my modern Maryland dentist surrounded by pretty girls and air conditioning.

Generations of Appalachians, stuck in a cycle of poverty, often lacked adequate food, warm winter clothes, medicine, physicians, and, of course, dentists. When my practice was finally established, I yearned to help the similarly deprived people in the world's most remote regions. Those lost in time like the folks on Nealy Ridge.

Foundational to my many overseas treks over the years were the endless string of adventures and misadventures that I experienced during my adolescent summers. I trust that the reader, in tolerating a sidetrack into a couple of them, will not be disappointed.

Now close your eyes and imagine yourself sitting on a rough-hewn, split-log bench perched precariously on a rickety front porch. Picture an Irish jig mated with an ole Virginny reel. Listen to the strumming of fiddles, the picking of banjoes, and the clacking of spoons while feet clog with joyous abandon in the sultry air of a southern summer evening...

Thirteen

UNCLE JOEL

Of all of Mom's siblings, Uncle Joel was my favorite. Somewhat short and stocky with a mischievous twinkle in his eyes, he was all belly and no butt; a family trait that I inherited along with thin hair. He was likable and always lent a helping hand to folks who were down. When he and Thelma wed, they bought a modest two-bedroom house on a pleasant knoll near Saltville, Virginia. Its short gravel driveway emptied onto Route 11 while the back looked at the mountains.

The town was named for the salt mines that preserved meat for the lean Southern soldiers during the American Civil War. (My kids just groaned. "Not the Civil War, *again!*") In the early 20th century, two foreign industries, British and Yankee, moved to Saltville to take advantage of low taxes, which boosted the local economy.

During the two-day drive from Maryland, we'd pull off for lunch at one of the burned-wood signs proclaiming: Picnic Table Five Hundred Yards on Left. Sliding into the fixed bench was risky; splintered wood awaited your fanny. And if we didn't balance ourselves on them, the whole contraption might tip over backward.

A few stops boasted two tables, allowing strangers to visit and swap lies while the kids ran off steam. Yellow jackets buzzed around open trash barrels looking for jam or sweet lemonade. Mom always brought a plastic tablecloth along, "For sanitary reasons." It was a lot more fun than an overcrowded food court.

After a day of crawling through every little Podunk town with the occasional traffic light, we'd pull into the mom-and-pop Valley Motel near Lexington. If there were no vacancies, we'd go on to Natural Bridge, which boasted high-price lodging to gaze at George Washington's signature on the stone arch. Today he'd be given a stiff fine for defacing a national treasure.

After being cooped up in the backseat of Dad's Buick, which was adorned with fins that could impale, Lee and I headed for the pool, little more than a concrete swimming hole. Mom and Dad would sneak off to the lounge for liquid relaxation and a Lucky Strike. I don't remember ever seeing Mom smoke; it's not that she didn't, but I never saw it.

Arriving the next day at Joel's, we'd spend a few nights so Dad could muster the courage to attack Nealy Ridge's treacherous mountain road. The jug of moonshine Joel kept hidden in the shed out back helped.

Although Uncle Joel had heartily welcomed my father into the family, he was quick to exploit his big-city ways. "Harry, yer one dumb, son of a bitch Yankee. But yer all right in my book." Joel's laughing face, wrinkling high to a receding hairline, suggested that somehow that was a compliment. "Come outside and sit a spell. Take a pull o' this 'ere *cider*, Harry. You boys grab a stick and whittle; here's my pocketknife, Carroll."

He eventually gave me that knife, which I still have—a prized possession. And despite the depredations into which Joel led his brother-in-law, Mom enjoyed our brief visit.

Uncle Joel's home boasted conveniences little known on The Ridge: indoor plumbing, a private telephone line, a Frigidaire, gas range, and washing machine with power ringer. A new Sears & Roebuck catalogue was proudly displayed on the coffee table.

For Thelma's birthday, Joel replaced her old clothesline with something that resembled a naked beach umbrella. She complained and he got her a gas dryer.

Joel gave Clyde a second-hand British Triumph long before he was of legal age. "What the heck, he's drove tractors, trucks, 'n' hay wagons. 'Bout anything on four wheels." Clyde hadn't earned the money for it, which raised a few eyebrows among the scratch-a-living-out-of-the-soil folks and fed gossip around the local dry goods store.

"That kid of Joel's is spoilt rotten."

"How come he done buyed a foreign job? Never find no parts fer it."

"I heerd it's always got 'lectrical trouble."

"Dumb as a brick outhouse when it comes to his kid."

Dark and handsome, Clyde cruised through town like hell on wheels, picking up girls. He soon totaled the Triumph. No one was hurt, and Joel just laughed it off. "That boy's sumthin' else." A few cars later, Clyde had to settle for a rusted-out Ford Fairlane, which he never totaled. It was the only vehicle that survived his adolescence.

Settled into a cane rocker in front of his Main Street haberdashery, Joel would shoot the breeze with any passerby. He knew a little about everything; just ask him.

He sold clothes. It didn't have to be clothes; he could sell anything. Joel was a born wheeler-dealer; a mountain boy who made good. Joel could hawk a Bible to a preacher man. "The only authentic version ta'en straight from the original Hebrew, verily spoke by our Lord His-self." Now, Jesus mostly spoke Aramaic and the New Testament was largely written in ancient Greek. But Joel didn't know that— or care. He seldom attended church, despite Grandma's untiring efforts to save his soul from perdition.

Regular customers were treated like family and given a fair price, but not the man whose forebears hadn't fought for "The Lost Cause." A Yankee accent and haughty air insured top dollar. "Pardon me, good sir. Might you have a sporting shirt appropriate for fly fishing?" The guy might as well tape a sign on his forehead: Please empty my pockets.

The flatlander might leave in a three-piece suit with reversible vest, patent leather spats, crossed suspenders, and a linen kerchief to match the starched button-down with all of it capped off by a fancy fedora. Having long forgotten the fishing shirt, he was sure that he'd negotiated a great discount. Joel had an uncanny way of making a "foreigner" feel special while he fleeced him.

Joel's standing in civic organizations was solid, nurtured by a keen business acumen. But everyone knew he'd been a highland hell-raiser. Thelma disapproved of drinking and after they were married, Joel swore off liquor. She was the love of his life, and he gave up the party once he saw the good of it. Except for that jug in the shed. Maybe she knew about it, but he was discrete and managed to maintain the fiction of sobriety for her and the Saltville Temperance League.

Thelma ruled the roost with an iron fist, which made the clan a little uneasy. Women just didn't do that. And she was an Abingdon flatlander. The family was never happy with the match.

"Why couldn't that boy marry a Chadwick?"

"Or even a Counts?"

"That woman thinks she's better 'n' us."

"Well...she ain't."

This pressure might've contributed to Joel sneaking a few belts now and again. Or maybe Joel was simply born wild. Either way, the marriage years were the happiest of his life. I was eight years young when Thelma unexpectedly passed on.

Joel's untamed nature hadn't prepared him to play both mom and pop, a twist of fate that left two hell-raisers to watch over each other. He became Clyde's friend rather than a father. "Wanna go play cards and get drunk?"

"Sure 'nuff." Clyde had it in his genes.

Devastated, Joel handled Thelma's death by draining his jug and spending lavishly on a grand funeral. She lay in state in a side nook in their living room. The casket sat on a gurney with ugly wooden blocks wedged under the wheels so it wouldn't take off on its own. Furniture was shoved against the walls to make way for folding chairs so folks could stare at her and contemplate the afterlife. The dining room table was covered with fried foods so mourners could eat their way through the wake. Thelma's flat-lander family showed a modicum of dignity while Joel's wailed like stray cats. Mountain folk do like their *goin' home* celebrations.

Thelma patiently waited for two days while surrounded by extravagant flower sprays, not the handpicked wildflowers common at Nealy Ridge funerals, but expensive store-bought ones. Her waxy hands were folded just so with a lily interlaced between her fingers.

Joel's home boasted a coal-fired furnace in the cellar, unlike at Grandpa's house, which was heated with hand-chopped wood. Heat rose through a cast-iron grate in Joel's living room floor. An outside hatch led to the cellar, which was permeated by lung-retching coal dust. Only the brave dared descend into that dark, damp world of spider webs and snakeskins. Rodents, their droppings everywhere, scurried along the stone foundation at the sound of an approaching stoker, or kids. Foreboding and sinister, it enticed curious young lads.

After filling up on goodies, Bart, David, and I spent the early evening catching fireflies out back. Getting bored, but having no desire to mingle with a bunch of old folks on death watch, we ducked into the cellar and quietly closed the double hatch overhead.

It was pitch-dark at first. But with the help of a faint glow filtering down through the floor grate, our eyes soon adjusted.

Before the wake, Mom and Aunt Aida had admonished us, "You boys behave respectful and reverent." We weren't sure what reverent meant, but the gossip in the living room didn't seem so.

"She never loved him, not really," boomed a female but masculine-like voice.

"Why on earth she ever married him, I'll never know," another meekly agreed.

"In it for the 'citement, I guess," a quorum echoed, which was ironic because Thelma had never been fond of Joel's mischievous ways.

"Well, his life is certainly one thrill after another! That boy was always gettin' in ta stuff he hadn't ought to," the first voice thundered loud enough to wake the dead (i.e., Thelma).

"Been almost too settled since she married him." Everyone had tried to rein Joel in, but when Thelma succeeded, she was faulted for it.

"He was full of vim and vigor afore her. But now…he's a gelding if ever I seed one," one biddy declared.

I turned to Bart and mouthed, "That's a horse with no balls." David looked down at his crouch.

"Nary a truer word spoken. What's he gonna do with his-self now?"

"I don' know, but he's got ta watch out for that boy a his. Clyde worries me. Reminds me too much of his pa."

We got an earful while they trashed the dearly departed, not yet cold and lying right there. Even to us kids it didn't seem right. "Ghosts don't take kindly to mocking," David whispered. We quickly left that subterranean haunt, sorely in need of some clean night air.

"Let's have a smoke." Not exactly fresh air.

"But we ain't got none."

Corn silk wrapped in old newsprint is not the best of smokes (it's probably the worst), but it'd do in a pinch.

I took a long drag…and coughed uncontrollably. Bart, an accomplished smoker, just grinned, his face framed by a perfect smoke ring drifting in the light of a full moon. I tried another puff but dizziness set in. I retched something green then went to bed early.

Evening turned to daylight; the aroma of a big, country breakfast floated down the hallway. At first I couldn't stomach it but managed to choke down a biscuit smothered with gravy. Thankfully, the victuals stayed put.

Mothers have the knack of magically producing neckties. After a mighty struggle to clip one on my collar, I filed onto the side porch with my cousins. The porch was protected by a tin roof in case of a passing shower. Our eyes remained respectfully fixed on the floor, which I noticed was rotten in places and sorely in need of paint. Aunt Thelma had been rolled from the parlor and the wood blocks secured so she wouldn't spill off the edge. Her empty shell looked surreal in the morning mist that hung thick over the proceedings.

Irregular rows of easy chairs, folding chairs, straight-back chairs, and kitchen stools sat on the lawn, which swept up to form an amphitheater. Bordered by the cornfield, there was plenty of standing room on the lawn for any passing neighbor in need of a good wail. All in all, it was a nice setting for a funeral.

For some unfathomable reason, I'd pocketed a slingshot and Bart had tucked a pet frog in his shirt pocket.

"Why'd you bring that wart-covered thing?" I whispered.

"Thought he might like to see a funeral. What's the slingshot for?"

"I dunno. Jus' in case." *In case of what?*

We sat with the immediate family on the porch and under the stern eyes of the congregation's funeral gaze. It wouldn't do to fidget, which might encourage Bart's frog to jump free. Clyde kept a steady eye that anchored us in place, his mischievous look long gone. My mind briefly wandered. *I wonder what it'd be like to use a frog in a slingshot.*

The rising sun soon chased away the morning fog and shined brightly on the mournful gathering. The pastor, tall and lanky and dressed in black, walked slowly onto the porch and hushed any residual prattling. In time-honored tradition, he read the liturgy—and then extensively elaborated on it. There's no such thing as a short-winded southern preacher.

In all likelihood he was self-ordained (another peculiar mountain custom), but that didn't matter. His opening salvo was fire and brimstone. Everyone knew what the Good Book says about sinners. I felt guilty thinking about putting the frog in the slingshot that poked my buttocks as the pastor turned to gaze upon the family. I slouched low and managed to sit motionless while it stabbed me.

Unable to compete with the happy, heart-warming sun, the preacher shifted gears from damnation to the assurance of Aunt Thelma's eternal reward. "She was the embodiment of everything kind and good and loving in a faithful spouse." I noticed the three biddies from last night's gossip fest squirm and avert their eyes. "She faithfully served the church and the cause of charity." That evoked nervous coughs from the jury of three. "The community has lost a valued and much-loved soul." She could do no wrong; Thelma had taken on sainthood.

The balding preacher got further worked up and reached for new heights by not so subtly bringing Thelma's wayward husband into the picture. It seemed that her every breath was divinely ordained to lift him from the gutter of satanic depredations and redeem his soul for all eternity. With stern admonitions from Leviticus, yet without a hint of henpecking, she'd led her alcoholic mate to forever swear off the bottle—or jug, in Joel's case.

My poor uncle looked grief stricken and…maybe a little hung-over?

The pastor's nasal pitch rose ever higher. Tears freely flowed, and I thought the weaker sex might swoon. The cadre of men who had gathered on the very same porch to smoke cheap cigars and toast Joel's libation liberation the night before shifted uncomfortably in their squeaky, hardback chairs. After commending Thelma's soul to eternal bliss, the itinerant parson called for sinners everywhere, especially those in attendance, to repent.

He invited those wishing to pay their last respects, and final farewell, to do so now. The summer sun had begun to beat down relentlessly and Bart and I had long since grown tired. We eyeballed each other, then boldly stood and strode confidently up to the open coffin. Bart gave Aunt Thelma a quick peck on her unnaturally waxed forehead and looked at me as if to double dare. I gave her a longer smooch. Bart seemed impressed as we stumbled down the rickety porch steps.

We quickly escaped into the cornfield. Once hidden among the maturing rows, we shed those tight black shoes our mothers had forced us to wear. We rolled a few corn silk cigarettes, and I promptly got sick—again. Nasty stuff. As my brain swam, the sweet melodic strains of "Amazing Grace" wafted through the carefully cultivated rows. Maybe God was trying to tell me something about smoking. I never took it up.

Uncle Joel was never the same. Although he remarried, Thelma would forever remain his bride. And despite all his theatrics, the parson did get one thing right: Joel needed Divine guidance. Family and friends relentlessly worked on him until he was baptized in the creek below Nealy Ridge. And he finally swore off the jug.

Unfortunately, his second wife also beat him to the grave. Joel again lost his way and once more took to heavy drinking. I was much older then and missed the kind, generous soul that I'd known growing up. But it counted enough that I named my youngest son after him. In his early fifties, Joel died of a heart attack precipitated by cirrhosis of the liver, lonely and alone. God doesn't want it that way.

Fourteen

OLE LINCUM

Stan and Gill, two buddies from dental school, came to Maryland for a weekend hike up Sugar Loaf Mountain.

"It doesn't get much better than this," Gill said with a grin.

"You got that right." Stan huffed and puffed as he stopped to catch his breath in the rocky terrain. "Carroll. You're a redneck, right?" I ignored him; he was just trying to be funny. "So, how many blacks do you have in your *southern* practice?" I stopped climbing and looked back down. On reflection, I realized that my practice was very cosmopolitan, including my employees.

Over the years I've hired a Muslim, a Jew (adopted by holocaust survivors), an Irish, a Pennsylvania Yankee, a Korean, and several Brazilians and hillbillies. Kate is of Swiss-French ancestry with a little Cherokee. I'm Scots-Irish, English, and Welsh and maybe a little Melungeon, whatever that is. Generational Americans are all mutts. Abraham Lincoln said, "I like a Mongrel myself, whether a man or a dog. They are the best for every day."

We'd never hired anyone of African heritage, but none ever applied; it just worked out that way. However, plenty of black folks have been patients for thirty-plus years.

"I don't know, Stan. I haven't thought about it."

Apparently he had. "I've got *only* one." Stan smugly held up a single finger, assuming a southerner would relate. But I didn't. Prejudice is a thing of the heart, not geography. I'm happy as long as folks trust me, show up on time, and pay their bills. However, our odd exchange got me thinking about my childhood visits to Virginia.

A hard stone's throw beyond the cornfield behind Uncle Joel's house there lived an old sharecropper who everyone called Ole Lincum. It never crossed my mind that his name was actually Lincoln. The old part was obvious from looking at him.

Joel and Lincum were good neighbors. "Hey, Ole Lincum. Can ya split me a cord o' wood? Give ya two dollars. US silver certificates. Two-fifty if ya have it laid up by Saturday," Joel might offer with a warm smile. The wood always appeared a day early, stacked neatly in Joel's woodshed.

An honest, trusting soul, Lincum never asked for payment. Uncle Joel would promptly pay after he snuck out to get his jug and discovered the wood. He always gave Lincum fifty cents extra for a job well done.

Ole Lincum's mammy was a slave of eight or so (no one knew exactly) at the time of emancipation. Suddenly set adrift in a world that didn't want her, she survived on odd jobs and eventually married. Although the new couple might've found steady work up north, her husband was afraid to go. "I'se told them Yankees eat black babies." It was a rumor spread by antebellum planters to keep slaves off the Underground Railroad. Southwest Virginia was all the world they knew. The last of their large brood, Lincum was named after the Great Emancipator. I never knew his last name.

When I was a mere whippersnapper, Ole Lincum was already about to break Methuselah's record. He had a sparse receding hairline, a scruffy beard, and tufts of white hair that sprouted from his ears. His withered fingers bent in directions fingers aren't meant to, evidence of advanced arthritis. Supported by a homemade birch cane, he walked with a pronounced stoop.

One lazy eye forever rolled about; it never blinked, and to look at him straight on was impossible. He wore patched overalls and a threadbare plaid shirt; the standard uniform of farmhands, black or white. His boots, fastened with frayed cotton twine, had been resoled several times. Lincum's humble abode boasted a wood floor, an improvement over the packed dirt with which he must've been familiar as a child. But hard rains penetrated the leaky hovel.

Like any Southerner, he spoke with a guttural drawl that exuded a warmth enhanced by his broad toothy grin and a twinkle in his eyes. Well, at least the good eye shined. Everyone, especially kids, loved his company. He was one of my favorite relatives, and I did think of him as an uncle. Uncle Remus personified.

Speaking of Uncle Remus, I think he's been wrongfully stereotyped. We do need to discard the insulting racial overtones of Mr. Joel Chandler Harris, but the anecdotes carried over from West Africa are anything but offensive. These clever yarns are akin to *Aesop's Fables*: they can be instructive or nonsensical but fun anyway; a rich heritage of sub-Saharan cultures mixed with a little Native American lore. We still read *Grimm's Fairy Tales* without thinking Nazi Germany. Why not Uncle Remus? My kids loved "Br'er Rabbit and de Tar Baby" as much as "Hansel and Gretel" or "Robin Hood."

But I digress.

While perched on a stump in his front yard, Lincum showed me and my cousins how to sharpen a blade and flip the business end of a knife into a tree. Despite his rough arthritic hands, he could still throw like no one else; and he never let pass an opportunity to show off his skill.

Bart had purchased a beautiful knife that cost him a week of mountain wages. "Whadda ya think of this, Lincum?" The old geezer gently passed his calloused thumb down the sharp blade and then checked its balance on his forefinger; he nodded while one eye rolled. Satisfied, he grasped the tip and without standing up whipped Bart's pride and joy at a huge oak tree. It hit with a *twang*, burying deep into the trunk. My irrepressible cousin pulled hard to retrieve his Sword Excalibur while David and I stared in amazed disbelief.

"Ya'll youngsters wanna' l'arn ta throw, proper like?"

"You bet."

"Well, now, fust time 'round put it in summthin' soft, like maybe da ground. Can't miss, 'cept dey's rocks and such might dull it." He squinted at Bart. "Only toss ole rusted ones inta the dirt. A hid rock kin chip a blade."

The old man sensed Bart's trepidation. "Nary mind dat. Da sharpenin' stone'll keep you boys outa trouble." He grinned slyly. "I heerd that ain't easy frum yer rep'tation up on da Ridge."

Eager to test our mettle against him, we sheepishly mumbled, "OK."

After several end-over-end tosses, the knife began to stick more often than not, which pleased our tutor.

Bart, ever the cocky one, boasted. "This ain't so hard."

Lincum saw the challenge and decided to make things more interesting. Although good-natured like Joel, he could be relentless—also like Joel. "OK, Carroll. I want ya ta stand over thar and spread yer feet fer apart. Real wide like."

I respectfully obeyed and stood spread eagle. Lincum sauntered to the other side of his scratch yard and suddenly turned, whipping the Bowie knife at me. It stuck into the ground underneath my crotch. I'm amazed I didn't wet myself. At least, that's my claim.

"Ya done good, boy. Didn't move nor nothin'."

Didn't move! I was too damn scared to move. He stared straight into my eyes while walking toward me, shaky from the pain of gout. With effort he held onto his cane and pulled Bart's big knife from its agrarian scabbard. "Stay put, youngin; this game ain't over."

Game? What game?

With a groan born of age, Lincum pushed himself upright and then pointed at the spot where the blade had pierced the earth. "Move one o' yer foots to thar."

"What?"

"Move 'em closer, boy."

It didn't matter which foot; both were equidistant to the scar. After reluctantly shifting, my stance was now half as wide. Ole Lincum hobbled back to his starting point, turned with a speed I believed impossible, and let loose the lethal weapon.

Thud! It struck deep. I stared incredulously as the knife quivered between my tennis shoes. *Wish I'd worn boots.* Lincum ambled over and, with another arthritic tug, yanked it out. Straightening up, he looked hard into my eyes with his one good eye. In the meantime, Clyde and Lee showed up but kept in the background, knowing better than to compete against the old sharecropper. Clyde's subtle smirk suggested that he sensed my fear.

Lincum ordered me to "Move dat foot agin."

I hesitated. *Is this supposed to be fun?*

"Go on now, boy. I ain't never missed. Well, thar was dat one time..." His eye gazed into the past while the cloudy one aimlessly searched. "But nar' you mind 'bout that."

I was scared but couldn't lose face in front of my cousins. The next round left my shoes only inches apart. I coughed up the courage to ask. "When's it gonna be my turn?"

Lincum grunted. "Don't trust the likes o' you. I'll chance it when ya git more practice."

I gulped when the bright stainless steel buried itself exactly midway, leaving little room to further close up. Lincum grimaced sideways. "Well, guess dat's 'nough fer today. Ya'll go on and practice. T'morrow I'll learn ya'll a game whar ya kin not hurt nobody."

Bart slid his prized knife into the leather sheath that hung proudly on his belt while I sighed with relief. He punched my shoulder. "You shoulda not looked so scared."

I glared back. "What're you gawkin' at?"

"Nothin'. Jus' glad my blade's OK."

"Ole Lincum 'ill knock you down a peg or two tomorrow." I hoped.

"I'm gonna wear heavy boots and jeans." Bart was cocky, not stupid.

On the way back to Joel's, we practiced throwing knives at a tree trunk. After a while we actually hit it, sometimes with the pointy end. Standing off to one side in tall uncut grass sat an old, forlorn picnic table. I don't remember ever eating there, although we'd sometimes plop down on it and jaw a bit. "Hey, let's flip it on its side." David wanted a bigger target.

Two hours later, we abandoned it to splinters. The following fall, back home in Maryland, Lee and I shredded our parent's picnic table into kindling. Dad was furious.

We avoided Ole Lincum over the next few days and took advantage of the stolen time to practice. But the dog days of summer were long, and the inevitable couldn't be put off forever. Feeling pretty good about our newly honed skills, we headed for Lincum's shack wearing the heaviest boots and thickest pants we could scrounge up. Lincum wouldn't miss, of that we were sure. But what if he insisted that we throw against each other? Better to be padded.

Lee had gone to town with Clyde to fetch store-bought cigarettes. So only Bart, David, and I walked across Lincum's yard, three abreast. Scrawny chickens scattered at our approach. The wizened old man was sitting on his rickety front porch, slowly rocking and whittling. Lincum glanced up and went back to carving who knows what—probably just passing time.

"Hey there, Lincum," we nervously called out.

The rocking and whittling stopped. He looked up with an unnerving grin. "Ya boys all ready?" Bart looked at me; I looked at David; David looked at the chickens; and the chickens looked at no one in particular.

"Sure am, sir."

A black man was seldom addressed as *sir*. His eyes narrowed to look deep into our souls and saw no slight, as none was intended. To us, the man was family; we honestly respected him. But on that day, a little healthy fear was thrown into the mix. Wise and perceptive with years, Lincum relaxed. Our training continued. "Awright then. Let's have at it."

Oh God. Why didn't I take up smoking like all the cool kids? I could've been in Saltville with Lee and Clyde, green from inhaling good Carolina tobacco but out of harm's way. We'd spent hours sharpening old knives (Bart had made a point of leaving his new one at home.), and learning their balance. But I still wasn't so sure.

"In dis 'er game, no one's gonna throw no blade at no one. Keep it real safe like." Us kids breathed a collective sigh of relief. "All ya gotta do is jus' what I does." It sounded easy enough. "Fust, I'm gonna toss my knife straight inta da groun'. Then ya'll does the same."

"Yes, sir."

Whoop thud. Each one of us nailed it, easy. Hitching up my pants, I strutted about with the chickens. I didn't know it yet, but Mumblety-peg is one game you really don't want to lose.

"Now, we gonna hang da pointy end from our nose and flip it. Stand up tall so's it has fer 'nough to drop. Den ya repeats da fust throw." Different, but not hard.

The third toss from the chin was essentially the same as from the nose. Bart mouthed off, "This is a cinch," and swaggered around the yard like a peacock, one-upping the roosters.

Next it was placed atop our heads, point down. By properly whipping head, hand, and weapon forward in tandem, the knife flipped and stuck into the ground. That's a little trickier; and it hurt my scalp.

As a variation on a theme, we progressively placed the point on each fingertip and flipped it. Not so bad; fingers have calluses, unlike my head. After a number of rounds, I found myself searching for a fresh spot.

We worked through all ten fingers, both palms (it helps to be ambidextrous), and elbows and shoulders. The routine stretched ever longer and no contestant could miss a single shot. If he did he was out and had to watch, humiliated, from the sidelines.

Toward the end, the knife was tossed over each shoulder with enough force to stick into the rocky soil. First David failed (actually on one of the easier throws), and then Bart on the harder over-the-shoulder throw. Lincum never missed. I managed to persevere.

Around the World was the grand finale. You must contort in such a way that your arm circles your neck and the knife sticks in front of you. Lincum demonstrated. Despite his painful arthritis, he nailed it. It was my turn. The knife stuck and I smiled. *Tied with the master*! But then it slowly tilted and keeled over. I was disappointed but thought, *Second place ain't all bad.*

I was about to find out why the game's called Mumblety-peg.

Ole Lincum ambled over and picked up my weapon. Upon straightening up, he sported a twisted, almost sinister smile. "We'll, boy. Now comes da true test."

A chill ran down my spine, but I managed to fake a reciprocal smile.

He pulled a sharpened peg—about the size of my little finger—from his overalls and handed it to me. "Carroll, you take dis an' push it inta da groun'. But only fer 'nough to keep it upright." That peg is what he had been whittling when we first strolled up to his porch.

Lincum unraveled the checkered scarf around his wrinkled neck and struggled to get down on his knees. "Put dis over my eyes and tie it 'round my head. Nice an' tight now, so's I can't see nuthin'." This was getting a little weird. "Don' be 'fraid to pull hard, Carroll," he commanded. I gave the knot an extra tug.

This old black sharecropper, the humble son of a former slave-girl, was about to teach me a life lesson. He pulled a small maul from a loop in his overalls and blindly felt for the peg sticking out of the ground. His once-powerful arm raised the hammer high and brought it down with a force that belied his infirmities. The maul stamped a deep impression in the dirt, right beside the peg.

"You missed," I crowed.

"OK, smart aleck. But da winner of Mumblety-peg gits t'ree whacks. Den da loser gots ta yank it out wif his teef." My face drained pale. Grinning, Bart and David leaned in. I prayed for Lincum to miss. *Whap.* Count two had only grazed the peg. My mouth went dry as he raised Thor's hammer the third time and hit the peg square, driving it below the scratch yard surface.

"You got it," Bart exclaimed.

"Man, that thing sure disappeared," David said gleefully.

"OK, boy." Lincum took the blindfold off. "Go on now; pull it out wif yo' teef."

As I kneeled, he pulled my hands around my back and tied the scarf around my wrists. That's when I noticed the chicken poop—everywhere. It'd always been there, but I'd never given it a thought.

Until that moment.

OK. Let's get it over with. My teeth attacked the crap-caked soil, found the peg, and clamped down on it. I even forced a grin around the grime-encrusted stick.

The victor nodded his approval with his good eye twinkling; he liked a good sport. Lord knows how many times he'd lost to skilled peers in the past. The filth I spit from my mouth mattered little compared to his warm endorsement.

I lost the match but learned the lesson: play the game and take what comes with grace. I continued to play Mumblety-peg with Lincum and my cousins. I've eaten more dirt in my time than I'd like to think on.

Ole Lincum came around Uncle Joel's fairly often. Sometimes just to visit, and sometimes to see if any odd jobs could be had. My uncle, greeting him with a warm smile and a hardy pat on the back, could always scare up a chore or two for his white-haired neighbor. Like Lincum, Joel came from a desperately impoverished background and knew he could use the ready cash. Although he had become a successful proprietor of a clothing store, Joel never forgot what it was like to be poor.

Aunt Thelma invariably emerged from the kitchen with a basket of fresh-baked biscuits, cakes, or maybe a jar of preserves; but always with a warm smile. Good neighbors, good folks.

But ugly prejudices lurked beneath this veneer of familiarity. I never once remember seeing my surrogate black uncle inside Joel's home. I'd been in Lincum's any number of times. "Cummon in and have some hot co'npone. Sit yo'self down thar, Carroll," he'd offer while motioning to a rickety, three-legged stool. But he was never invited in to rest on Joel's easy chair, or even to sit outside on the front porch rocker.

And the wizened old man always came to the back door, never the front—an unspoken rule. I can picture him through the screen door, standing out back and patiently waiting, as if white folk existed on an inherently higher plane. To my discredit, it took me twenty-odd years to realize this terrible injustice. I discovered prejudices within that I'd never claimed.

It was just the way of things.

But that didn't make it right. And no number of excuses will ever make it so. Honest introspection can be a harsh schoolmaster. The pill was especially hard to swallow in light of how much I loved and respected Lincum.

So when a Yankee friend makes a sideways racial remark, I'm not so quick to judge. He's wrong but I'm just as guilty. Better to clean up your own house first. Only God's love is unconditional; a Truth that levels the playing field.

I miss you Old Lincoln. And I'm sorry.

Fifteen

HORSE VS. CAR

They say you can never go home again. That's not entirely true. Memories of Nealy Ridge flooded back to me when my family moved to Gloyd; the sad-looking barn, outbuildings, and the two horses that conveyed with the house were reminiscent of The Ridge.

Tuffy was a chestnut-brown quarter horse; she stood about fourteen hands. The other was a magnificent sixteen-two Thoroughbred named Alimony; Dick had purchased him from a man desperate to catch up on his ex-wife's payments. Tuffy came with a saddle and a bridle. However, there was no tack for Alimony.

A Saturday in mid-April dawned overcast as wind gusts blew hard across the fields. Kate's dad drove up our lane with a present to brighten the dreary morning: a used bridle, blanket, and saddle. All were pretty ragged, but Alimony, nicely groomed, might make them look good; *especially with me riding him.*

Confidence: "The feeling you have before you completely understand the situation."

I found a cobweb-covered halter in the barn, hid it behind my back, and walked into the barnyard. As I slowly revealed it, Alimony snorted and shied.

"He's gonna be a hard one to catch," Frank called out.

"Don't worry 'bout me." I stepped boldly forward and... Alimony pranced out of reach. For several minutes I chased him in circles, which worked about as well as you might think. *Maybe bribery?* His ears went forward as I gently sifted a bucket full of sweet grain through my fingers. Alimony followed me, or the bucket, into an unfinished box stall in the half-finished barn and settled down to munch on the treat. I decided to ditch the halter and go straight for the used bridle Frank handed me. Surprisingly, Alimony stopped eating long enough to take the bit without a struggle.

The saddle blanket should be easy. But when I tossed it on his back, he freaked and shot sideways. The blanket hit cockeyed, slid off his hindquarters, and landed on the dirt floor where Alimony sprayed it with nervous manure. After several more attempts, he pinned me against the timber walls. Although unnerved, I was determined to win this struggle between man and beast.

"Jus' get the saddle on 'im. Forget the blanket," Frank directed from safely without. I grabbed Alimony's reins as Frank continued to encourage me. "OK, you've got 'im now."

But it didn't feel like I had him. "Why don't you get in here, Frank?"

"Don't yell. You'll rile him and he might hurt himself."

"Him? How about me?" Alimony's nostrils flared, and his eyes wide-wild.

The large horse finally settled down and let me deftly slip the sodden blanket and old saddle on him. As I cinched up the girth, there was a loud *snap*; the strap had broken. In a psychotic frenzy, Alimony reared high, sending the unbelted saddle into a fresh puddle of runny manure. At the other end, his flailing hooves barely missed my face.

"Watch out," Frank shouted!

"Thanks for the warning," I grunted while scrambling to avoid a half ton of chestnut muscle. Retiring to opposite corners,

Alimony and I warily eyed each other. The saddle was useless without a strap and pretty gross, like the blanket. But I was determined to ride the crazy Thoroughbred. My only option now was bareback.

He calmed down—again—or maybe he was as tuckered out as I was. I led him from the barn and brought him alongside the fence where I handed the reins to my feather-weight father-in-law. A good snort from this charger could send Frank flying across into the next county. However, I had no choice but to trust him.

Cautiously, I climbed the fence and swung my right leg over Alimony's bare back. He reared up, his forelegs pawing the air. Now, I hadn't held onto a mane since I was six, but it saved me from tumbling off and breaking a bone, or my pride. I set my knees in a viselike grip while Frank tossed me the reins and the diablo steed bucked in circles. He calmed somewhat when he felt the tug on the bit.

I only wanted to walk and ever so slightly touched my heels to his quivering flanks. He bolted. Bred for racing, the feisty Thoroughbred had no inclination to walk or even trot. It didn't matter. Galloping into the gusting wind, I was thrilled to be riding for the first time in years; bareback heightened my adrenaline rush.

As we turned back toward the barn, Alimony settled in to a smooth rhythmic gait. Frank noted that I sported an ear-to-ear grin, although I nearly collapsed upon dismounting. My wobbly legs were not accustomed to riding. Alimony needed a real saddle; or maybe I did.

When we bought the farmette, I thought Dick's western saddle was too pricey but now swallowed my pride and drove over to our old Pyleton townhouse to beg the beautiful hand-tooled leather saddle. I paid top dollar for it. As I struggled to get the bulky treasure, along with a really cool bridle, into my station wagon, Dick declared, "Ya know, Alimony's got ta be handled with care."

Still irritated at the high price, I curtly fired back, "Why so? He's no problem." I wasn't about to tell him about our battle in the barn.

"He was jus' broke by a wrangler. Not been rid since las' fall," he drawled.

I had unwittingly ridden—bareback—a powerful, partly crazed beast that was green! A chill ran up my spine. Angels *do* watch over children and fools.

In the end, Alimony turned out to be a great ride and quite a jumper, but only when in the home field. On the trail he shied at everything: birds, rabbits, squirrels, stray leaves, and a discarded soda can. He was terrified of groundhogs.

We came to a mutual understanding: he went where he liked, when he liked, and as fast as he liked while I rode along. My only other choice was to remain behind, sprawled on the ground. We stuck to that arrangement as long as I owned him.

The barn sat in a side field, enclosed by an unpainted three-board fence. However, the smaller front pasture was defined by only a few lonely posts; no fencing. I ordered more locus posts and oak boards to nail to the posts with the help of anyone who happened by: my father-in-law, mother-in-law, friends, and Mom. Tara and Russell began making themselves scarce whenever I headed outside, hammer in hand. People eventually stopped visiting. My brother only came at night. Desperate for help, I tricked Lee by firing up the Coleman lantern so we could work late into the evening.

The Pyleton Polo Club captain checked in from time to time. "Folks with building projects don't seem to have any friends," he said with a smile.

When Stan came down from Joisey to see our new homestead, I introduced him to fencing. "Working in the fresh air's a lot more fun than in a cubicle." He eagerly chipped in—the Huck Finn affect. Stan and I finished the little that was left to do and he laid claim to building most of it.

Along the country road, a weathered mailbox sat on a locust post where the gravel lane started its climb to our house about five hundred feet away. In order to rotate pastures we led the horses across the driveway, a thirty foot divide. Tuffy easily cooperated, knowing that the grass was, in fact, greener on the other side. But Alimony hated to be led around by the nose, despite the promise of fresh grazing.

The young stud, sensing freedom, pranced through the first gate; but in the open divide he became obstinate: rearing, bucking, and generally being a nuisance. He had to be strong-armed into the front pasture, a chore that typically fell on my broad shoulders. Kate, Tara, or Russell always handled Tuffy—except one time.

On that one occasion, Alimony easily cleared the near gate but started yanking Kate's rope. She did OK until a rope burn caused her to momentarily relax her grip. Recognizing an opportunity, Alimony broke free and whinnied triumphantly, spiriting toward Stabletown Road. My heart skipped a beat when he dashed across the tar and chip surface to run wild across the way.

At first a dispassionate observer, Tuffy soon got her dander up and gave me a rope burn to match Kate's. With superhuman effort, I shoved the mare into the front field and slammed the gate on her hindquarters, which she defiantly kicked at.

"We need to catch Alimony before he gets hit by a car," I yelled while running down the drive with Kate hard on my heels. Tuffy ran alongside us inside the fence.

In the meantime, our errant equine was having a good time in the fireman's scorched field. When he heard Tuffy neigh, Alimony galloped recklessly back across the road.

"Good, he's going home," I shouted to Kate. But then he suddenly turned toward our neighbor's picture-perfect farmhouse.

Howard, a retired metalworker, had been born in that house and still lived there with the devoted wife of his youth. His beautiful garden was the envy of neighbors. I'd established a small patch in honor of my father who loved raising vegetables. But my garden soon became a weed-infested jungle just on the other side of the fence from Howard's. It was a *Better Homes and Gardens* before-and-after picture. I eventually plowed mine under and put in a swimming pool with water that is sometimes greener than the garden ever was.

Now our harebrained horse was headed full steam for Howard's Eden. Without a moment's hesitation, Howard dropped his rake to help catch him. However, having made a beeline for the salad bar, Alimony was already trampling Howard's ripe green beans and budding tomato plants. Creeping squash vines became entangled in Alimony's legs.

Howard had a corn field in the far corner; not the hard feed corn common to our area but tender sweet corn. Alimony disappeared into its neat rows, his progress marked by waving stalks. We tried to box him in, but he eluded capture by what looked like moonwalking.

Realizing that he'd have no respite to peacefully graze, Alimony raced out through an undefiled patch of veggies, leaving yet another path of destruction. Although upset for Howard, I had no time to stop and reflect. Our crazed animal might cause an accident and seriously hurt someone if not soon corralled.

A trash truck came along and saw Alimony trotting proudly alongside the road. It jerked to a stop and a father-son team hopped out. "Need some help?"

"Sure do," I panted. But the extra manpower was to no avail. Alimony, seeing the enemy increase in number, again bolted for the wide-open spaces across the road. Unable to help, the Good Samaritans continued their rounds while I fretted.

He'd been running loose for a good half hour and Kate and I were exhausted. The sun sank low in a sky blazing in reds and oranges outlined by turquoise. I prayed that the blood-red glow was the good omen portended by sailors.

"Watch him while I get some grain," I shouted to Kate while racing up to the barn. I returned, huffing and puffing. Alimony, probably a little tired himself, paused when he saw the familiar bucket. His ears twitched forward as his eyes fixed on it.

Just then, headlights approached from the other side of the hill. I ran into the road, boldly waved, and yelled, "Stop!" At the same time Tuffy, having also seen the bucket of sweet oats, neighed. "It's time to stop horsing around and come home for dinner," she seemed to say. Alimony whinnied in reply, set his back hooves, and ran full tilt toward home.

In my mind's eye, everything now transpired in slow motion.

A small sports car cleared the crest and slowed when the driver saw me. Alimony reached the pavement at breakneck speed and tried to stop but on his slick horseshoes he skidded hard into the front left fender. The momentum carried him onto the hood, up the windshield, over the roof, and then rolling off the trunk to land splayed on the pavement. The sound of crunching steel and breaking glass reverberated in the dusk.

Oh no! Alimony's killed himself!

But I was wrong. He scrambled upright and ran toward Tuffy who was going nuts. Kate, anticipating his move, was already racing up the lane. She barely beat him to the gate and frantically opened it. Alimony sailed through as she quickly slammed it shut and secured the heavy chain. "Whew! That was a close call!"

Close! What about the people in the car? Its top was flattened to the doorframe. Sickened at the sight, I forgot about the stupid horse and ran over to the squashed car. "You OK in there?" Our horse had half pushed it off the road.

A shaky voice faintly squeaked back. "Yes…I…I think so."

"Are you alone?" I tried to see through the shattered windshield that was flattened over the dashboard and front seat.

"I…uh…yeah." Although confused, he was at least alive but stuck inside.

"I'll pull on the door while you push." It groaned before suddenly springing open to spill the driver onto the asphalt. I gave him a hand up, and he leaned against the shattered fender. I gave him a quick once-over in the faint light of rapidly approaching darkness; he seemed to be in one piece.

"Can you walk? Our house is just up the hill."

"Yeah, just give me a minute." Still dazed, he staggered up the steep drive without too much assistance. The young man wore English riding boots. "I planned to ride at an indoor rink up in Barnesville this evening." *Thank God, he knows horses.*

Under the bright glare of our kitchen lights, we further searched for injuries and found only a few bruises. He explained, "I quickly laid down on my side when I saw him coming." He'd avoided serious injury, or even death, by so doing. But in all likelihood, a few premature gray hairs would soon sprout.

We sat around the kitchen table and exchanged insurance information. "Our horse is totally responsible," I offered. "I don't really need your insurance info." Although gracious, he understandably wanted his car fixed.

"Thanks. I just need to call a friend to come get me." He was ready to go home. After hanging up the phone, the man tried to stand. With a wince and faint groan, he dropped back into the chair. "Something's cutting my foot."

I pulled his boot off and tipped it upside down; out poured a stream of broken glass, jangling melodically as it hit our tile floor. The old sports car didn't have safety glass. He shook his downturned head and mumbled, "Horses can be so stupid."

He was probably in shock when we had walked up the hill and hadn't felt the glass. I would have been after seeing a thousand pounds of brown coming at me. Now able to walk comfortably, he and I set off to see about his car before it was hit again.

We peeled a bit of canvas from the convertible roof and pried up the windshield frame so he could scrunch into the driver's seat. The car started and ran fine except for a screeching noise that echoed in the stillness of night while slowly going up the driveway. He parked it and sat down on our back stoop to wait for his friend. "Thanks for all your help," he said with a crooked smile. *He's thanking me?*

The following morning dawned crisp and bright. After downing several cups of black coffee to jumpstart my brain, I headed out for work. But the smashed car in our parking lot (a rude reminder of the previous night's waking nightmare) jolted me awake in a way the coffee had not. "Wow. What a mess," I muttered.

It lent a junkyard atmosphere to our new, yet unfinished home. The front left headlight was gone, while the fender, hood, windshield, door, roof, and trunk were battered beyond belief. It was a miracle that anyone—including the horse—had survived and equally amazing that the car had been somewhat drivable.

During our busy work schedule, I stole a quick break to call our insurance agency. The cheerful operator patiently listened to my rambling without comment and then excused herself. "Hold for a minute." Without covering the phone, she shouted, "Hey, everybody, it's the guy with the horse!" In the background, her office roared with laughter. My unfortunate friend had already called the insurance company. That's when it dawned on me how truly bizarre this was. Our homeowner's insurance took care of everything.

Early the next day, a rusted tow truck arrived. A burly, tattooed driver hopped out and sauntered slowly around the sports car for a good once-over. He paused and removed his greasy baseball cap emblazoned with a catchy logo: *You smash 'em. We trash 'em.*

Furrowing his brow, he scratched his balding head and squatted to better examine the damage. Pulling clumps of chestnut hair from the cracked-chrome trim, he asked, "Hey, buddy. What the hell happened? Hit a deer?" He examined the hair in his hand. "Must've been a big one."

"Nah, some crazy horse got loose." In the distance Alimony neighed and proudly pranced around the field while I turned to rush off to work.

That evening the sports car was gone, but the spot was marked by shards of broken windshield. I bent over and picked up a battered Triumph emblem before shuffling up our back walkway. A grocery bag sat on the bench outside our kitchen door. Holding no grudge, Harold had given us some vegetables that he'd salvaged.

I carried them inside and announced to Kate, "I love this town."

Sixteen

LOUISE

With our increasing work load, Natalia was being run ragged. Kate, still home with baby Joel, couldn't help yet. Although I'd trained both of them, I now wanted a board certified assistant; I could only chance so many root canal fires. After much coaxing, Natalia agreed to man the front desk full time even though it was not her first love.

A pleasant sounding lady with several years of experience answered our ad. "I can stop by first thing tomorrow morning," she told Natalia over the phone.

"Good. How 'bout eight-thirty?"

Louise arrived at 8:15 a.m., a half hour before Natalia. At least I was already in the office. In her mid-thirties and smartly attired, she was attractive and knew her way around an operatory. After marrying her college sweetheart and working for a few years, Louise had stayed home to raise her preschoolers, a commendable attribute. When her third kid entered public school she worked part time for a large multispecialty practice, learning a little bit of everything. Louise could easily fill-in at the desk when Natalia cut out early on those beach Fridays.

She grew up in Kentucky bluegrass country and loved horses. I hired her on the spot! The only downside I could find was her infatuation with Neil Diamond, who she'd once met backstage. She was positive that he'd written "Kentucky Woman" just for her.

On Louise's first day, I asked Natalia to keep our load light so Louise could familiarize herself with our equipment. It's like a buying a new car: you know how to drive but still have to figure out which knob is for the headlights and which one is for the wipers. Even then you might panic the first time it rains. Case in point:

When the county injunction had stopped construction on my office, the landlord allowed me to lease his suite one evening a week. But I was restricted to the treatment room with old equipment with which I was not familiar. It was better than nothing.

I seated my first, and only, patient that evening and clipped the bib around her neck. Topsy was one of the few folks who had followed me from Dr. Dolph's office. She probably had a proper name, but I never knew what it was. Her chart just said, "Topsy."

"Just sit back and relax," I said as much to reassure myself as her. "This won't take long."

I pushed the button to recline the chair. Nothing happened. *This is embarrassing.* The mouth light wouldn't go on. The foot pedal didn't work the drill and the air/water syringe wouldn't squirt. *Must be a master switch somewhere?* But I couldn't find it.

"Uh, I'm not sure how to turn this old thing on, Topsy." I blamed the equipment.

She sprang to her feet, tearing the bib from her choker chain in the process, and joined me in the hunt for a switch. Topsy immodestly crawled around on all fours; something wiry older women with sun-leathered skin shouldn't do in short skirts. She soon discovered a lever on the base of the chair.

"Here it is, Dr. C. I think it's a toe kick."

A tough old bird, Topsy hammered it with her palm and everything came to life. With a sly smile, she sat down. "You can work now, Dr. C." Topsy was a great sport. Remembering Stan's fiasco with his falling X-ray machines, I gave her a discount.

But now I had moved into my modern office. And despite plans to keep things easy on Louise's first day, several emergencies were squeezed in. It became one of my busiest days—ever. With virtually no time for a decent lunch break, everyone on staff had to grab a bite on the run. Kate was able to help in the morning but had to leave by midday to pick up Joel at the sitter's.

With both operatories filled, the waiting room was often standing room only. Kate and Louise barely had time to disinfect and set up rooms up for the next patient. Natalia wanted to help in the back but with the phone ringing off the hook and folks crowded around the reception window, she couldn't. The place was a zoo.

When time permitted, we showed Louise where supplies and instruments were kept and where dirty instruments could be temporarily stashed out of sight. "They can be sterilized later," Kate explained. However, patient treatment can't be rushed; that's never an option. So when Kate left, how did we manage?

Louise. The new kid eagerly jumped into the fray, sorting through the clinical demands as best as she could. And she exuded a calm, soothing aura for patients while doing it.

Around midday I stole a precious moment for a few bites from my pitiful, brown-bag lunch: PB&J and greasy chips. I was in mid chew when Louise came hightailing down the hallway, a fistful of dirty instruments in hand. Screeching to a halt, she looked me dead in the eye. I was horrified, thinking that she was going to tell me to take this job and shove it.

Instead, she placed one fist on her shapely hip and declared, "I really like the tempo around here."

I nearly choked. But there was no hint of sarcasm. *I'll let her know later that this isn't normal.* But I didn't on that today. Instead I gave her a quick heads-up on the afternoon patients—especially the quirky ones. A little background helps us relate appropriately to individual patients and meet their expectations. Louise listened attentively, obviously valuing my input.

While I talked, she put the dirty instruments aside, washed her hands and retrieved a bag of baby carrots from the frig. Louise's robust stature belied her delicate eating habits, which were in stark contrast to petite Natalia who consumed double her weight for lunch.

Topsy, who was scheduled for midafternoon, might be a logistical nightmare. Although nice, she could prattle endlessly about her numerous medical ailments or the latest fad in homeopathic remedies, none of which had anything to do with dentistry. If she didn't have maladies brewing, which was almost never, she might drone on about her neighbor's pet's rare disease.

"Hey, Dr. C. I bet you've never heard anything like this: Ms. Hockmeyer's cat has a big blind spot. Can't see where it's going. Walks into everything."

"That's nice, Topsy. Now, what seems to be wrong with your teeth?"

"Vet can't figure it out but still charges a pretty penny for a half-blind cat."

"OK, Topsy. But you're tooth problem—"

"You wouldn't believe it. Runs right into the road an' never gets hit. Cat's not worth a plug nickel. Can't even get itself killed."

"Sure, but getting back to your—"

"Damn vets charge the same for a stray feral as a good mouser."

I would lose focus by the time she got around to the dental crisis of the moment. With the day's unusual time constraints, I anticipated getting farther backlogged while trying to feign interest in one of Topsy's endless monologues.

Being incredibly tired during my briefing with Louise, I let my guard down. Flippantly, I suggested that Topsy would likely show off a fresh scar from her most recent operation and want everyone to take a look. A close look.

"With today's luck, it'll be on her skinny butt," I blurted out before thinking it through. *Did I say that out loud?* The shock on Louise's respectable, southern-lady face told me I had. And she didn't know if it should be taken literally.

"You're joking?"

"Maybe. I sure hope so," I mumbled sheepishly, embarrassed.

Quickly recovering her composure and professional demeanor, Louise marched off to help treat the next three or four patients.

Then the dreaded moment: Topsy arrived. Her loud, raspy voice (from smoking far too many cigarettes for far too many decades) carried above the general din. "Tell the doc I'm ready for him."

Natalia didn't look up. "Have a seat, Topsy. He'll be with you as soon as he can."

"My appointment's right now, young lady!" Topsy had so much to tell and so little time.

Desperately needing a break to gear up for Topsy, I retreated to my office while Louise called her back. I was guzzling some caffeinated soda when my prim-and-proper assistant came crashing unannounced through my door marked Private. Tears streamed down her rosy cheeks.

What has Topsy said to offend this poor girl?

But she was laughing; so hard she gasped to catch her breath before announcing with a Cheshire grin, "Topsy had an operation just like you predicted, Dr. James." Her eyes sparkled.

"And?" I prompted.

"She had a large mole removed—"

"Not so bad," I interrupted.

"From her butt!" Louise squealed while wiping her face. "She dropped her pants in the operatory to show me the scar!"

Topsy was never the shy one.

I shuffled into the operatory, relieved to see Topsy seated in the dental chair with her pants on and the confining bib securely fastened around her neck. With a pleasant demeanor, I reached out my hand in greeting. I really did like the old gal. "Hi, Topsy."

She looked up, smiled broadly and, ignoring my proffered hand, pushed the bracket table aside and jumped up.

"Hey, Carroll. Wanna see my new scar?"

But it wasn't really a question. Before I could answer, she'd dropped her drawers; slacks and grandma undies breezed down as one.

At such times, a doctor has to pretend interest and sympathy all the while maintaining decorum. But it was difficult to keep my cool with the new employee cupping her mouth with one hand and trying to stifle a laugh in the background. I couldn't hold back any longer and quickly turned to leave.

"I...uh...forgot something, Topsy. Be right back."

I practically sprinted down the hallway with Louise close behind. It was obvious that Louise and I were going to get along just fine. Our funny bones were aroused by the same shenanigans! We later discovered that we had many more traits in common.

Louise continued to arrive early and work through lunch when needed. For years she remained a valued assistant and always a friend. But my brain is forever stuck with that vision of Topsy's bony derriere.

Seventeen

HORSE BOARDING

After completing the siding on our unfinished house, I built bedroom closets that Halfway Dick had neglected to construct. Our congenial neighbor, Harold, told that he had walked the house while Dick was in the middle of construction and asked him where the closets where. Dick had forgotten to include any. Kate wouldn't hear of me tackling anything else before she had a place to hang her clothes.

"I'm using the back of a chair," I grinned. She was not amused.

We discussed ways to get additional money for the materials. I would provide the labor. "How about boarding a horse?" Kate suggested. My dad had boarded several when I was growing up in Potomac so I figured I was an expert.

"Not a bad idea. But I have to finish the barn first," I insisted. It was only framed and covered in plywood without siding, roofing, or doors. That would take more money.

Kate, Tara, and Russell helped install roof shingles, board and bat walls, and Dutch doors along with three finished stalls and a tack room.

A fixed ladder led part of the way up to the un-floored hayloft. Secured by a couple of vertical two by sixes three feet apart, its rungs were horizontal two by fours nailed at appropriate intervals. The bottom step was perfectly level with the concrete floor. (The stall floors remained dirt.) The next was spaced and placed as it should be. The third was *almost* the same distance from the second and not quite horizontal. *Not so bad; it's just a barn.*

However, the rungs became more random and cockeyed as the ladder rose. It looked like a kid's tree house. The project had been abandoned about halfway up. I finished it, but left the helter-skelter steps as a tribute to the founder of the farm.

Dick's King Cab F350 was emblazoned with a magnetic *Southern Comfort* banner. Rumors circulated Gloyd about Dick's drinking. One could determine, with a reasonable degree of accuracy, the amount of spirits he'd consumed at any given time by critiquing his workmanship.

But at least we now had a hayloft. Mr. Earl Bail, a retired county employee who lived on a nearby farm, would call sometime in the middle of July. "I'm cuttin' and balin' next two days. Give ya a good price if ya git it straight from the field." He always used the same line. "Jacks up the price if I have ta put it in my barn first."

I'd drop whatever I was doing and recruit Tara, Russell, or Kate—whoever failed to make him or herself scarce. While following Earl's baling machine through the blistering hot fields, we'd pile our small pickup so high with hay it threatened to topple over while negotiating the rolling hills.

But gathering hay under the relentless sun was easy compared to stacking it in the new loft where temperatures could reach 110 degrees; it's sweaty, nasty work. The kids learned the true meaning of "Make hay while the sun shines."

With a functional barn and two pastures, we were set for a couple more horses.

I've never had show horses. Shampooing, braiding manes, and blacking hooves were never who we were. But the animals were always well cared for. In the freezing winter, we'd trek out twice a day to give them a bucket of oats and toss hay into the manger. But when grass was plentiful, we just let them graze.

In looking for a like-minded renter, I made the mistake of advertising in a large Washington newspaper. A polite but somewhat snobby man called. "Good afternoon, sir. I am seeking a moderately priced establishment in which to board my very expensive, purebred racehorse."

"We have a modest farmette in Gloyd that—"

"Is there an indoor ring in which to exercise him?" he interrupted.

"Uh, no, just a three-stall barn and open field. But there are plenty of wooded trails around." A purebred racehorse wasn't what I had in mind.

"And what about other horses? Might one be diseased?"

"We vet ours regularly, and there are no other boarders."

"Would he be properly cared for in the rain and snow?"

"The barn is tight." I was proud of that fact. "He'll have a stall in crappy…ah, inclement weather."

After extensive interrogation (he let me know that he was a lawyer), he still expressed interest. My asking price was right. He naturally insisted on a full inspection of our facilities to make sure they were adequate—and safe.

I gave him easy to follow directions; easy for anyone but this guy. "So, you think I should turn after three miles?"

"Actually, you turn after three *and a half* miles, like I said; you can clock it."

"Now, you're suggesting that I make a right turn at the stop sign."

"No. I'm not *suggesting* it." I was getting a little impatient. "If you don't go right, you won't get here." We finally agreed to meet out by the barn early on Saturday morning. *I wonder if he'll be able to find the barn.*

On Friday afternoon I asked Tara to help me spruce up the tack room for the upcoming inspection. Toiling in the heat while sweat poured down our faces, we pounded eight-penny nails to make shelves and saddle racks. Two of our horses wandered into the barn for shade; our fields lacked trees.

Suddenly, there was the sound of whinnying and scuffling of hooves. "What's that noise, Dad?" Alarmed, Tara stopped working; it was quite a ruckus.

"Probably nothing. Maybe a little spat to challenge the pecking order." But to reassure my daughter, I left the tack room to check it out.

Tara followed just in time to witness her new mare violently kick up with newly shod hooves, catching Tuffy's hind leg wedged between the sturdy oak wall and the concrete floor. Like breaking a tree limb with your foot, Tuffy's leg snapped; a bloody bone protruded from the gaping wound.

Tara dropped her hammer as Tuffy's blood-curdling, agonizing cry pierced the stillness of the hot afternoon; it was echoed by Tara's own otherworldly scream. The surreal pandemonium will forever echo in my brain.

Tara remained frozen in place while I chased her horse from the barn. "Go on. Git outta here," I yelled at the culprit. Turning back to Tuffy, I hoped that I'd seen it all wrong.

I hadn't. "Tara! Run and get Kate. Have her call Cherry Tree Veterinary."

Tara shouted while dashing toward the house. "Kate…help… call the vet!"

After placing the call, Kate ran out to see for herself. When she saw Tuffy, her pained expression mirrored my own feelings; there was no hope.

The vet soon arrived and led the limping beast outside to better inspect her injuries in the waning light of a setting sun. After consulting a colleague in Leesburg, Virginia, he hung up and informed us: "She has to be put down. It's hopeless." We already knew that.

Before administering the lethal injection, he walked Tuffy to the far side of the barn where her corpse wouldn't be seen from the house. It was pitiful to watch her struggle along in such pain. Tara, Kate, and I turned and shuffled sullenly through the barnyard while he euthanized Tuffy. As a simple matter of decorum, he placed a horse blanket over her.

I had not a clue how to dispose of a half-ton of decaying horseflesh. But the vet had already thought of that.

"Carroll, I wrote down a number for you," he offered with compassion in his voice. "They open at seven."

Tuffy was Russell's horse. Although Tara was the more natural rider, Russell had worked very hard with Tuffy to become proficient; he wouldn't take this well. It was getting late and there was nothing left to do except call him at the beach where he was vacationing with his grandmother. After our heartrending talk, I settled in for a long, morose evening. Dinner wasn't on my agenda.

While staring into space, darkly reflecting on the day's events, I suddenly realized that the pretentious racehorse owner was due first thing in the morning to inspect our safety standards. And I'd neglected to get his phone number in case something came up. *Might be a good idea to get rid of the dead horse.*

But the horse morgue didn't open until 7:00 a.m. All I could do was call and hope for the best! Anxiety further drove the swirl of emotions coursing through me.

Following a restless night, I actually awoke with a calm feeling. "Things are gonna turn out fine," I muttered while dialing the phone not one minute after the hour.

Then a perky operator cheerfully announced, "Good morning. Valley Protein!" It was a *dog food* factory! Russell's beloved horse was destined for poodle chow!

I'd started to recite directions for the much-too-upbeat receptionist when she interrupted. "I'm terribly sorry, sir. We can't *possibly* have a driver there today. The earliest would be Monday."

"Monday!" *This...cannot...be...happening.* The lawyer was due any time, and the carcass would soon start to smell in the intense heat of July. "I'll pay anything extra," I pleaded.

"I'm truly sorry, but we're backlogged. Nothing can be done until Monday."

Despondent, I dragged my sorry butt out to the barn while having delusional thoughts: *Maybe I can hide the body.* When I turned the corner, I stopped short and gasped. Tuffy's legs were reaching for the sky; rigor mortis had set in. And her morbid salute had pushed the blanket off.

She was on the side of the barn that faced the road, giving a clear view of her bloated body from Stabletown Road. It would be even easier to see her while coming up the driveway. In a surreal daze, I tried forcing her legs back under the blanket. Nothing short of a chainsaw would do. (No, I did not seriously consider it.)

I anxiously trekked back to the house, plopped down in front of the TV, and stared at the blank screen, having neglected to turn it on.

"What're ya watching?" Kate walked into the room and looked at the silent screen.

"Nothing. Go look out by the barn."

She soon returned, her face reflecting my own disbelief. "Whadda we do?"

"Wait...I guess."

Midmorning came and went. Lunchtime passed.

Figuring that racehorse guy got lost, I wandered outside and saw a *Jaguar XJ16* about halfway up our driveway; it was slowly backing down. He'd finally found us and probably already figured his horse wasn't safe here.

I sighed and moseyed back to the house but began to run when the telephone rang. It was Valley Protein's driver.

"I'm thinkin' 'bout coming tomorrow," he said with a raspy smoker's voice. "Have ya'll got a Catholic church nearby?"

"Sure do. There's a nice country church a few miles up the road." *A church graveyard for Tuffy might be nice.*

"That'll work out. See ya tomorrow," he said.

"Thanks." I hung up before telling him where to find the body. But not to worry, all he had to do was follow the smell.

Early on Sunday morning, a heavy-duty pickup announced its arrival with a roar; black diesel smoke spewed from its chrome stack. Out climbed a burly man in faded overalls, Wellingtons, a threadbare flannel shirt, and a camo hat perched high on his forehead. A cigarette dangled from one corner of his mouth.

Walking out to greet him, I was hit by the rancid odor of decaying meat; he'd already picked up a dead cow, black with hungry flies. *Maybe the smell of tobacco helps him get through the day.* Noticing that vultures, or something, had attacked the cow, I examined Tuffy who was thankfully still in one piece.

The truck was modified for the purpose. When opened, the tailgate could be lowered by hydraulics and a dead animal ignobly dragged onto it with an evil-looking hook attached to a steel cable wrapped around a motorized winch.

The driver cheerfully chatted away as he placed a leather harness around Tuffy's torso, attached the hook and pulled a lever; the winch groaned.

"Can't tell ya how hard it is to keep help; that's why we're backed up." He pulled a second lever and the tailgate flipped Tuffy's body against the cow with a sickening *thud*. "Last guy quit after jus' a week."

Go figure! Assuming he'd already attended Mass, I casually asked, "Any more stops, or are you going straight back to Hagerstown?"

"Nope. I'm headin' up to *your* St. Martha's." He grinned.

I had a nightmarish vision of him pulling into the parking lot with his ghastly load. Smiling parishioners, dressed in their Sunday finest, held the hands of tiny tykes who sniffed the pungent air while adolescents laughed at the welcome diversion. I pictured the driver hopping out with a smile. "Good morning y'all. Dr. Carroll James of Gloyd sent me!"

Kate and I decided against boarding horses.

One morning a couple years down the road, I saw a neighbor coaxing three horses into our front field with a bucket of grain.

"What's up, Brenda?"

"Your horses got loose. I knocked on your door but no one answered. Thought I'd just put 'em back."

"They're not my horses," I explained. "But go ahead. We'll try to find who they belong to."

"I'll ask around, too." Brenda smiled while smacking the last one through the gate.

Kate located the owner who didn't know they were missing and no longer wanted them. We kept the large gelding, which Russell named Sundance. I'd sometimes double up on Sundance with Joel, but as Joel grew that got a little cramped, especially on trail rides. At age five, he needed a horse of his own.

I saw a notice in the country store for a free Welsh pony. A lady on a distant farm was looking for a good home for Dolly; her teenage daughter had outgrown her. I conveniently neglected to mention Tuffy's fate. Twenty-eight-years-old, Dolly had a great disposition. She was perfect for Joel, who soon became quite attached to her. Three horses and a pony was herd enough for us.

Another year passed and a beautiful spring morning dawned. The smell of honeysuckle wafted on a gentle breeze. Lovebirds chirped as Kate and I prepared for a ride through the ancient forest across the railroad tracks. We'd taken that Monday off from work, and the weather had cooperated perfectly.

After putting Joel on the school bus, we caught our mounts and led them into the barn. Dolly followed us inside but was acting weird, pawing at the ground and skull-butting us. It was so out of character that I soon became concerned and stopped grooming Sundance. I looked Dolly over but couldn't see anything wrong.

"Maybe age is catching up with the old gal," I suggested to Kate. "We'll phone the vet if this keeps up. But right now I wanna get going and not waste the day." Imbued with a little bit of Nealy Ridge self-sufficiency, I was never quick to summon the horse doctor.

Kate and I returned home from our long trail ride, exhausted but happy. Joel's pony greeted us like her old self, nuzzling affectionately for a treat, which confirmed my decision not to call the vet.

After a quick breakfast the following day, I headed out for the office and noticed vultures circling. Dolly's legs were sticking straight out while a swarm of flies buzzed around her torso. It was an all too familiar sight. As if to announce, "I told you I was sick," she'd expired next to the fence beside the lane.

I couldn't go to work before having a father-son talk with Joel, so I backed the car up our gravel driveway. He was almost ready for school, but I took him back into his bedroom and sat on the edge of the bed.

"Listen, buddy. Dolly passed away last night. I'm really sorry, but she was quite old. It was just her time."

He slightly nodded, taking the news quite well. With renewed confidence, I continued. "She wasn't acting herself yesterday. I was gonna call the vet, but she died during the night." Seemingly unfazed, he stood and finished getting ready for school. I gave him a big hug.

I knew exactly who to call before I headed out of the house a second time. The same pleasant receptionist at Valley Protein promised that a driver would pick up the corpse before Joel got home from school.

"Well, will you look at that," she exclaimed. "You're already in our computer."

Maybe I should put them on speed dial, I mused.

The dog food company, true to its word, picked up Dolly's carcass before I got home that evening. *Thank God for small favors.* After putting my briefcase down in the kitchen, I kissed Kate.

"How did Joel take it when he saw his dead pony lying right there by the driveway?"

"He was fine, holding my hand as usual while we walked down to the bus stop." But her sly smirk unnerved me. "He hesitated briefly when we came to Dolly's body, but then picked up the pace and marched on down without a word."

I had a sinking feeling but said nothing, not wanting to interrupt.

Kate continued. "The crowded school bus soon arrived, and I gave Joel a quick peck on the cheek." The door had opened with a *swish* and he'd deftly hopped aboard. Pausing beside the driver while gazing down the long center aisle, he loudly announced: "My horse is dead because my father wouldn't call the vet!"

Pudgy round faces plastered themselves against the dusty windows to get a glimpse of the carcass, which was easy to spot with its legs extended in that morbid salute my family was now familiar with. *Maybe that could be our farm logo.*

My reputation became mud at the elementary school: kids, bus drivers, teachers, counselors, and concerned parents of the PTA. I definitely wasn't looking forward to seeing my son that evening. Kate now had to comfort me.

I went into Joel's bedroom and tried to explain myself, but he just shrugged having already moved on. After proclaiming his dad's negligence to the whole world, Joel never again brought it up. Great kid.

But these days I'm a little quicker to call the vet.

No horses passed away during the writing of this story.

Eighteen

To Russia with Love
Or
Once Upon a Time in the Soviet Union

"*T*he church is seeking volunteers to join a two-week delegation to the Soviet Union," Pastor Winston announced from the pulpit, his Adam's apple bobbing in his slender neck. Tall and gangly with a high forehead that had outgrown his comb-over, he was Gloyd's own Ichabod Crane.

I've always been fascinated with Russia: its sheer size, epic literature, and grand music. Everything's big. *Bolshoi*. Lost in a Russian novel, I'd envision myself astride a mighty steed, racing across snow-covered steppes while a lonely village materializes in the crystalline distance.

Soviet visas required a black and white photo. In a small shop near DC's State Department, a jolly rotund lady took my mug shot. "Now, honey, don' you be smilin' for them Russians. They jus' want frowns." My picture resembled Boris Badenov's scowl. I lived with that ugly passport photo for ten years.

In 1988, the fifteen delegates of US-USSR Bridges for Peace teamed up to try and reduce Cold War tensions on a grass roots level. Previous teams had included civic groups, educators, churches, students, etc. Amnesty organizations need not apply. They were unwelcomed in the Soviet Union.

We met with former delegates to hear their experiences and sample traditional Russia cuisine like borscht, a beet soup. "Talks will be strictly controlled by the Soviet Peace Committee," Steve, our no nonsense coordinator explained. "Pravda means 'truth' and Izvestia 'news.' But a popular joke states: 'There's no pravda in the *Izvestia* daily and no izvestia in *Pravda*.'" That was as light-hearted as Steve got.

Kate made a great last supper: shrimp cocktail, salad, steak 'n' potatoes, warm rolls with real butter, and lemon meringue pie with a scoop of Breyers. This meal often came to mind during the following two weeks. In the excitement—or trepidation—neither Kate nor I could sleep. The heavy meal certainly didn't help.

That morning, our team drifted red-eyed into Dulles Airport. Kate grabbed all the cameras for a group shot. With fifteen straps wrapped about her wrists, draped over her shoulders, and choking her neck, she looked like a *paparazzi*.

"Aeroflot Flight 807 is now boarding at gate D-6."

There were many tearful farewells as we headed for a forbidden land and our nation's number one enemy. My smile faded as I hugged Kate goodbye. This was not a vacation.

The Ilyushin, a sad copy of a Boeing 727, was designed for much shorter hops than this twelve-hour marathon. And the Russians had packed in extra rows, which gave me a new appreciation for my short, Scots-Irish legs. Once airborne, an elderly team member stood and called from the back. "Hey, Doc."

I turned just as we hit an air pocket that almost upended him. "Whoa. Be careful, Bill," I grinned. "It's a little bumpy."

"No problem. I've flown worse." Bill was a retired photojournalist who'd traveled extensively. "I just broke a tooth on a nut. What should I do?"

"Does it hurt?"

"No."

"Then I'd wait till we get home to have it fixed."

"Good idea," he said with a gapped grin.

Lorne, an elderly church administrator, shouted to another team member, "Hey, Jim. You hear what they did when one of your fellow parishioners moved to our street?"

"Uh...no." Jim belonged to a denomination of skeptics.

"They burned a question mark on his lawn."

Jim grinned sheepishly, but I don't think he got it.

We flew through nighttime and into the dawn. Moscow's distant rooftops reached skyward through the early morning haze as we descended. I could barely contain my excitement when we touched down at Sheremetyevo International Airport, until I saw customs agents armed with automatic weapons. And I wasn't prepared for how young they would be. A guardian of the Motherland stared at my passport and then at my face, repeatedly. While several scrutinized our baggage—for several hours—Lorne exclaimed, "Well, Toto, we're not in Kansas anymore!"

We hopped a charter bus to the Hotel Ukraina, a dark foreboding building that was one of seven such Stalin buildings. Four harsh towers punctuated its corners while the center spike stabbed starkly at an overcast sky. Dark clouds swirled briskly about the black spires, accentuating an Evil Empire effect.

More armed guards inspected our papers at the entrance. Behind us, the nine-foot high door slammed shut; the *thud* echoed though the cavernous lobby. Stony-faced desk clerks in wire-rim glasses stood behind protective glass. It felt like a visit to see Uncle Vanya who was imprisoned for bootlegging vodka.

Clippiety-clop...clippiety-clop. A large lady in a plain suit and heavy platform heels, with hair pulled back in a tight bun announced, "Passports, pleeeaze." When she had to tug on mine (I hate giving up my passport.), her plastic smile disappeared. But I thought about all those persuasive AK47s and relaxed my grip. She snatched it with a huff. I never saw it again until we left, two weeks later.

The enormous, yet crammed elevators reeked of body odor and decayed teeth. Semi fresh air washed in when the doors opened, only to become oppressive again as they closed.

My roommate, Jamie, and I spilled onto the twenty-sixth floor where a beefy hall monitor shortstopped us with a jerk of her head. Small blocks of wood, chained to old-fashioned skeleton keys hung above a metal desk that was shoved against the wall. She perused our paperwork, muttered something in Russian and, with a glare that implied, "I dare you to cross me," handed Jamie a key. Unlike the bespectacled clerks downstairs, she wasn't protected by bulletproof glass, but she didn't need to be.

Jamie desperately fiddled with the door lock to escape her harsh glare. Our quarters were Spartan, with two tiny beds and one bedside table, but it was clean. Jamie's six foot four inch frame hung over the end of his bed. But at other hotels we didn't always get separate beds. The bathroom shower lacked a curtain, and the toilet lacked water. *How does this work?* I pushed a knob and water shot across a porcelain island. The flushing mostly worked.

Jamie was a young Episcopal priest with short-cropped hair who taught Russian history at DC's St. Alban's school. He was as anxious to see the sights as I, despite the clippiety-clop matron's directive: "Wait in rum; slep till meal. Feel beeter."

Paul, a Yugoslav expatriate who had written a book on Christian-Marxist dialogue, had been to Moscow several times and invited anyone interested to join him in a two kilometer walk to Red Square. Including Jamie and I, six team members went along. Our reentry pass was another wooden block with Cyrillic writing.

Several brazen young Muscovites kept pace beside us. "I like...would to trade shoes...rubles for sneakers." He gazed down at my feet. "Favorite, she is Nike." *Gee, the brand I'm wearing.* But it wouldn't do to be arrested for illegal trafficking on my first day in Mother Russia.

"Nyet."

Shortly after passing by the Arbat neighborhood, I exclaimed, "There it is!"

Looming large, as if from a Russian novel, were the rust-colored walls of the Kremlin, an imposing backdrop to Red Square. To the right was Lenin's Tomb and opposite were the colorful onion domes of Saint Basil's Cathedral. The Tomb of the Unknown Soldier brought to mind the horrors of WWII when even Stalin's religious persecutions were curtailed; Cathedral Square's churches were now just museums.

In 988 AD, Vladimir the Great forced a mass baptism in Kiev's Dnieper River. Church membership was mandatory, which set the tone for the 20th century when only party members could get a decent job or flat. However, in the interim, the Orthodox Church had become the soul of the people, sustaining peasants during the misguided politics of Potemkin the Charlatan, Rasputin the "Mad Monk," and sadistic rulers such as Ivan the Terrible and Father Joe's kulak genocide.

The biting wind that whipped through narrow medieval streets and swept down broad boulevards didn't dampen our spirits. Before perestroika and Gorbachev we'd never have been allowed to roam without an escort.

Back at the hotel, the lukewarm shower trickled and turned cold as I rinsed off. Jamie tossed me a towel and loudly complained. "These flimsy rags are full of holes." After a sumptuous meal in an elegant dining room, we returned to our room to find a clean stack of extra-thick bath towels. Our rooms were bugged!

After a sound night's sleep, we met with the Moscow Peace Committee. Like all subsequent meetings, it was carefully choreographed. There were different conference rooms and faces but always the same rhetoric:

"Welcome to worker's paradise."

"Plenty to eat?"

"Best food in world. Maybe France better?" A concession.

"Same for all comrades."

"Religious freedom number one socialist agenda." They played to our team's sensibilities.

"Ninety percent people vote in election."

"Yes, unlike capitalist West." Sadly, that was right on the money. But when Jamie pointed out that we had a choice, their English degenerated. "No understand."

"All peoples vote *da* or *nyet*," proclaimed one irate apparatchik. Of course, *nyet* could cost you your job, housing, or worse.

Day after day, boring soliloquies extolled the virtues of a worker's paradise—parroted noise. Only the intermittent sightseeing rejuvenated us. As honored guests, we took a special Kremlin tour. And the Moscow Circus is best experienced in Moscow. At the Bolshoi Opera House, we saw an opera based on a German fairy tale that was written by a Frenchman and sung in Russian. I dozed off but awoke to see the hero die and recover—several times—to wail something in Russian before finally succumbing. Bill and Lorne awoke at the final applause. Jamie enjoyed it.

We were isolated from the outside world. There was no access to international telephone service. Soviet TV showcased homeless Yanks sleeping on subway grates or insensitive Brits eating roast pork while the proletarian world starved. Kate received my one telegram only the day before I got home. To cut exorbitant costs, I abbreviated it. "Cold as *WT*." Her friend deciphered it and they howled laughing.

After a week in Moscow, we flew to Lvov in Ukraine. I took a short walk in a picturesque park near our hotel that first morning and was pelted by brisk gusts in the cold gray drizzle. But the locals seemed oblivious as they hurried off to work.

An old babushka held the hand of a small boy marching along in bright red galoshes. He was probably her grandson. Spotting a puddle, the boy suddenly pulled loose and jumped in with a splash of delight. Grandma scolded and lightly smacked his butt. He whimpered, but quickly recovered and skipped down the winding path. Even at a distance, I saw a slight twinkle in the old lady's eyes. It's what little kids do; they jump in puddles. And what grandmothers do—softly discipline.

I turned introspective. *This is ground zero. Nuclear warheads (Armageddon purchased with my tax dollars) are targeting them and me.*

Lvov, an ancient city of intricate stone architecture, is not far from the Polish border. Soaring spires, flying buttresses, gargoyles, and freezes of saints and cherubs adorned medieval cathedrals. Graveyards filled with crypts of long forgotten dukes and duchesses bordered parks that showcased mounted heroes. Quaint shops lined narrow cobblestone streets. I almost expected to see Pinocchio skipping along with Geppetto trudging behind.

Sarah, my fellow Gloyd delegate, who was blond and stout and a little younger than me, suggested that we take morning walks together to sharpen our senses for the day's work. One day we wandered too far afield and got turned around—a little scary in a place where few folks spoke English and an oppressive regime fostered distrust.

"It's getting late, Sarah; we should get back," I suggested.

"Yeah, I'm ready for breakfast. But which way?"

"I think it's this way." We followed a narrow street, lined with cast-iron streetlamps. It curved and dead-ended. A stylishly dressed woman emerged from the arched doorway of a townhouse and hurried down the worn stone steps. I desperately waved to her and asked for directions with a few memorized Russian phrases.

In British accented English, she emphatically announced that she was *not* Russian. "I am Polish, from an old family here in Lviv. We seldom speak Russian."

Lviv was the city's Ukrainian name. Embarrassed, I muttered, "Sorry. I don't speak Russian either."

"I could tell."

"We're Americans looking for the Hotel Lvov."

At that her round visage brightened. Americans were rare. "The enemy of my enemy is my friend." But we didn't feel like anyone's enemy; just lost souls in need of a friend.

"It's not far. Go two streets down and make a left. You'll see it," she said as she pointed.

"Spasiba…uh…thanks."

"Good luck…and welcome to *Lviv*," she shouted with a grin while rushing off to work. It was the first heartfelt welcome we'd gotten in the USSR.

Sarah and I briskly walked along an eight-foot-high stone wall that enclosed an Orthodox monastery that had not been destroyed by the Bolsheviks. Folks were pouring through the ancient entryway—young and old, male and female. We elbowed through the crowd for a glance at the cathedral within, and then squeezed back upstream and out the gate.

"Let's see if Kevin is back from his morning run," Sarah smiled.

Kevin, a lanky fitness nut, had smuggled a duffel bag full of benign religious literature into the USSR: Sunday school lessons, coloring books, etc. Such materials were considered illegal propaganda that carried steep penalties.

Back at the hotel, I pounded on Kevin's door. He opened it a crack, a bath towel wrapped around his waist.

"Hey; what's up Carroll?"

"We need your duffel at a crowded church nearby," Sarah exclaimed,

"Great. I'll be right there." Kevin had been waiting for such a time as this. We soon crammed ourselves into a packed St. George's Cathedral, which was standing room only, and inched along the back wall while quietly gesturing with pamphlets in hand. The congregants pretended not to notice us.

Finally, a young woman hesitantly peeked at my tract written in Cyrillic with a picture of Jesus on a hillside. Possibly the Sermon on the Mount? "Blessed are the Peacemakers…" Her eyes shifted nervously before she snatched it, keeping it at waist level. She slowly looked down and her hands began to quiver; a smile spread across her pale face, framed by a scarf. She glanced up and whispered, "Spasiba bolshoi." Thank you very much.

She quietly passed it to a friend who nervously nodded toward the duffel. Kevin gave her a booklet with Noah's Ark on the cover, which she showed to her three stair-step children. They gawked at the colorful animals filing in two by two.

As these two tracts were passed around, hushed tones slowly got louder until we were suddenly rushed. In the crush of a few electrifying, almost terrifying, minutes our entire stash was gone. With our duffel empty, we headed for the door while receiving myriad double-cheek kisses, hugs, and handshakes. There was a spiritual hunger that we'd been told didn't exist in the USSR. We were blessed far beyond our simple gifts.

A couple days later, our team boarded an evening train for Kiev. "The Soviets are afraid we'll spy on the countryside," Steve announced as the sun set. The tiny communal bathroom, with a waterless sink and toilet that opened directly onto the tracks, was in an adjoining car; we had to cross a coupler to get to it. It was a little exciting.

Despite the screeching breaks at every village and being crammed into triple berths, Jamie and Paul slept. Not me. In the frigid morning air, after eight jolting hours, we climbed down to the platform in Kiev and stretched our legs. As the sun rose brightly, someone began singing, "*Oh what a beautiful morning….*" All of us Americans spontaneously joined in, which brought disapproving looks from somber Soviets.

We milled around on the sidewalk outside our hotel while Steve went in to the lobby to check in. A youngish woman, neatly attired in a business suite, boldly struck up a conversation with Paul. "Who's up for going to a Pentecostal service with Tanya?" he announced.

Pentecostals in the USSR? "I'll go."

"Me too," echoed the group; everyone decided to forgo a nap and shower except Steve, who had to remain above reproach and stick with the official schedule.

Each of the three rusting cabs sported a cracked windshield that was missing at least one wiper blade. In the rigidly controlled economy, wiper blades were low priority. The driver reached outside to smear dew from his windshield when slowing, but never stopping, for red lights. The bald tires squealed every time he swerved.

"Why do you attend church so far away?" I asked Tanya, who had squeezed into the front seat with me.

"No one see. Underlings love snitch." A good job, nicer flat, and more vacation time were perks she could easily lose as a churchgoer.

The cab skidded to a screeching halt outside a drab, rectangular building that looked like a factory. *Maybe they used to make wiper blades here.*

"Where's the church?" I asked.

"Here. Please to come in." Crowds were gathered around the windows looking inside where it was already packed with parishioners. Our bold hostess forced her way through the throng, losing team members in the process. I got stuck in the center aisle. I saw Bridges people, scattered throughout, holding their cameras high to take blind shots of the crowd.

One elderly gentleman with random wisps of white hair sprouting from his head tried to talk to me. He first attempted Ukrainian and/or Russian, then maybe Polish, German, or French. Finally, he tried English.

"Where from?"

"America." That was a showstopper. People turned their heads to see me while excited chatter spread through the cavernous, ex-warehouse. They smiled and patted our backs while ushers came to lead us forward. Folding chairs magically appeared in front of the altar. We sat while so many had to stand. It was a little embarrassing.

Midway through the three-hour service, the pastor asked us to sing a hymn. To the delight of the congregation, we belted out a reasonable rendition of "Amazing Grace." Then the kids came forward for a children's lesson as part of the service, thereby circumventing the law against Sunday school.

We returned to our hotel where Steve patiently waited. I had noticed an army of babushkas sweeping Kiev's streets with straw brooms.

"Is this make-work?"

"Yes and no," Steve answered. "After the Chernobyl disaster, the city was sealed off until recently. The cleanup is to reassure the populace, and foreigners, that any residual radiation is being controlled."

That was about the time I started to lose my hair.

The following morning we met with the Kiev Peace Committee around a huge conference table. They touted the deep fraternal love between Ukrainians and Russians, which was blatantly false. Television cameras were trained on one Soviet who berated the West for distorting Soviet history. Jamie, who had a PhD in Russian history, turned bright red and stood up. He planted his white-knuckled fists on the table.

"If you'd stop altering your history every time the Politburo changes, maybe we could get it straight."

The translator hesitated. When he did speak, the apparatchik began to scowl. Everyone shuffled nervously in their seats until Jamie sat down. The head honcho made some lame joke and the meeting again became rote propaganda.

The Kiev Committee canceled our second meeting, substituting it with a meeting with tight-lipped university students. College was a precarious privilege. However, during a recess while everyone strolled aimlessly through the university's marble hallways, several English-speaking students struck up muffled one-on-one conversations.

"I like pick own job—teaching—but must study science," a studious-looking sophomore told me.

"I can't travel West Parents in weapons development," said another who glanced nervously around. "Not permitted outside country."

The monolithic communist wall had begun to show a few cracks.

Another night train delivered us to Moscow. Compared to the train's cramped berths, the Hotel Ukraina was like Shangri-La. We'd been forewarned that we might become depressed sometime during our mission. It hit me one drizzly morning when I slowly dragged myself out of bed. Jamie had already gone to breakfast when I rang our leader. "Steve; I'm sick." Not really a lie. I skipped the tours of *Izvestia* and *Pravda*.

During those meetings, Paul was approached by Yuri, a dissident who arranged clandestine meetings. Some of us volunteered to go with Paul later that evening. At that point, I had shaken the gloom and wanted to help make our mission more meaningful, although I'd miss the nighttime festivities.

Six of us, including Yuri, piled into one cab, which after about forty-five minutes stopped on a decaying side street. With trepidation, we climbed out and followed him past an unmarked white van with a whip antenna. Inside the van, a video camera was aimed at the decrepit apartment building we were heading to. It suddenly swung around and followed our progress with no pretense of secrecy.

A chill went up my spine. *This is nuts.*

A crumbling archway led to a passage poorly lit by a dirt-encrusted bulb suspended by a threadbare electric wire. Paint peeled from the walls while the metal staircase rusted. Incongruously, a new electric cord coursed up the stairwell into the first apartment on the right. Nervously, we climbed up to that same flat.

Yuri knocked twice and entered without waiting for an invitation. He exchanged kisses with Andropov, a thin, middle-aged man with a burly beard who'd recently been released from the Gulag.

The one-bedroom apartment seemed even colder within than outside. Our small cadre squeezed into the kitchen where Andropov's roundish wife sat on a three-legged stool beside a small table. A youngster wearing hand-me-downs clung to his mom's legs and looked up in wide-eyed wonder. Born soon after his dad disappeared into the Gulag, the disheveled boy had no early memories of him.

Several older kids lounged about in ill-fitting clothes. Propped against a wall or sitting on counters, they eyed us suspiciously. The eldest, his head shaved, stood with legs slightly apart ready for a brawl to defend his dad's honor.

After introductions, I inquired about the new wire in the stairwell.

"Did you just get a telephone?"

"For listening device," Andropov replied nonchalantly.

Now I'm under no illusions that my country is 100 percent compliant with constitutional guarantees—it's not—but that would make headlines. Not in the USSR.

Andropov's wife sobbed softly. When asked what was wrong, Yuri replied, "Because you here." Andropov gently patted her shoulder, but she would not be consoled, convinced that the men in the van would drag her husband off to prison as soon as we left. Under perestroika it was unlikely that we'd be arrested, but he was taking quite a chance meeting with us.

Andropov had suffered the horrors of labor camps for seven long years. Kevin asked what crime he'd been charged with. Staring at no one in particular he declared, "Imprisoned for illegal foreign contact!" *Exactly what he's doing now.* He was one of the unsung heroes who changed the world. Six months later he was featured in *US News and World Report.* He still hadn't landed a job and didn't qualify for state aid. But he hadn't been hauled off to jail again. And now his song had been sung.

On our second to last night, the Soviet Peace Committee planned a relaxing evening at a nightclub. Most of us wouldn't be there. Another foray into Moscow's forbidden suburbs had been planned, and our illicit numbers had climbed to eleven.

On the subway Yuri instructed: "Stay in twos and threes on different street corners. Hide cameras and jewelry. Don't look too Western." I looked at my Nike's. They were not made in Novosibirsk.

Paul and Yuri disappeared down a dark alley and soon returned with a young man who asked, "Where Americans?" Yuri discreetly nodded toward the four corners. Our contact shook his head and waved us in. "KGB arrest if want to."

While following him to an upscale neighborhood, I looked for a stake-out. I never saw one. We went to the contact's comfortable flat where we talked with him and his wife. Those young professionals were willing to take risks for human rights that we take for granted. They hoped to have kids one day and wanted them to grow up free.

Overly tired at breakfast the following morning, I was startled by a crushing bear hug from behind. Cool Sasha—our KGB babysitter was so nicknamed because of his steel, gray-blue eyes— asked with an emotionless smile, "So, Carroll. Why were you not at dinner last night? All of those in attendance had a wonderful time."

I pictured eleven empty seats around a banquet table and avoided looking directly into those demon eyes. "Not feeling well," I muttered.

"Many of you were sick last night. An upset stomach or a bad headache. A migraine I think you call it? I stopped by your room to see if you were OK."

I wasn't in my room! My knees became week.

"Are you OK now?" he smirked.

Flustered, I said nothing; my mouth had gone dry.

Sasha stared at me before turning to "chat" with another reprobate. It seems that Jamie had suffered the same stomach ailment. Sasha's penetrating glare stopped Jamie in his tracks, and few things rattled my roommate. I entertained unpleasant visions of a strip search and interrogation.

Sasha was the only Russian we'd met without a British accent; his inflections were reminiscent of my Michigan cousins. Sarah wondered how he'd learned such nondescript American English.

"Did you ever live in the United States? Maybe Chicago?"

"No, I learned it from a book," he glowered.

People don't learn accents from a book. But this operative was not to be trifled with. He was unused to challenges by "na-ive" religious folks who were hopelessly contaminated by "the opiate of the people." The Soviet Union was a scary place.

After fifteen exhausting days I was ready to head home. The westbound flight seemed longer until a Bridges delegate magically produced a harmonica. We killed time by singing songs such as "Home on the Range." Not one nostalgic American had a dry eye. The Russians on the flight thought we were all crazy.

At Dulles International Airport, one of our team fell to his knees and kissed the ground in imitation of Pope John Paul II. A customs agent smiled. "Welcome back."

Kate greeted me with a strangling hug and nonstop kisses. During the ride to Gloyd (she drove) we shared a few stories about our two weeks apart. She related details while I doled out one word answers.

"So how was the weather? Is it windy in March like here?"

"Cold. And, yes."

"Was the food any good?"

"OK."

"Did you meet any foxy women?" A test to see if I was listening.

"A few." I faked a sly grin. "Sorry, Kate, I'm exhausted. For the last two weeks I've been speaking through interpreters, which gave me lag time to think."

"OK. I'll do all the talking." And for the entire forty-five minute ride, she did. "Debbie and I got together and Eric came over. Russell's been riding and Tara's been busy with friends. Joel often asked about you. Mom had us over for dinner and…" But I enjoyed every minute of the home front news.

A month or so later, Kate was reading through my journal when she paused at a brief entry: *Can't get going. Tired of same BS. Lay in bed half the day.* Then she grabbed her diary. At the precise moment when I was depressed in Moscow, she'd sensed that something was terribly wrong and wrote in her diary: *Urgent prayer needed for Carroll.* Across ten thousand miles and nine time zones, our spiritual connection had remained secure throughout.

Somewhere in the dark recesses of the Russian Secret Service on Lubyanka Square there's a file on Dr. Carroll James of Gloyd. I get chills thinking about that.

It was good to be back in the United States.

Nineteen

A New Beginning

After returning from Russia, I continued to build our new home that we had already moved in to. It always seemed to be filled with construction dust.

"It's gonna take twenty years to finish this place," Kate chuckled while rolling primer on the bare drywall in our bedroom. It would take longer.

As I considered all the time, energy, and money we were putting into our three-bedroom home, I felt a little guilty when comparing our place to the cramped Soviet flats.

"Why don't we get something smaller," I suggested at breakfast one day.

"Then where would you put that home office we talked about?" Kate countered.

I knew she was right and proceeded to draw up architectural plans for converting the garage into a dental office. I proudly submitted them to Park and Planning. They were promptly rejected.

The clerk used red ink to mark all over my meticulous blueprints that had taken me untold hours to draw to scale with straight edge and T-square. "Now redo them like this." It took several more weeks, but I finally finished. Those were also rejected. I submitted a third draft to yet a third clerk. He spoke little

English but stamped them: "Accepted." I wished I'd learned how to say "Thank you" in Korean from Dr. Lee.

After hiring a plumber and an electrician (I did all the carpentry.) I managed to get an occupancy certificate, just as the money ran out. I had to make-do with second-hand furnishings just as I'd done with the Rockville office. An old file cabinet and my childhood desk were crammed into a tiny alcove that served as a business office. A worn out couch from Frank's contact lens and artificial eye practice filled the small waiting room. The garage floor was sloped, so the couch angled downhill. Folks waiting for their appointment instinctively leaned uphill. As they unconsciously squirmed in anticipation, they'd slowly drift south into their downstream neighbor.

Pencils regularly rolled off the kiddy desk, which I thought was funny. But not Kate. "I'm forever picking them up off the floor," she growled. To keep the peace, I shimmed the two downhill legs with wooden blocks. I found it less amusing when my instruments rolled across the bracket table, despite attempts by my supply man to level the second-hand dental chair. And my stool, along with the assistant's, would subtly drift as if possessed. I'd find myself stretching to reach the patient while my assistant crowded in from topside. It was all reminiscent of Dr. Frieden's office; too soon, I'd passed judgment on him.

But I was mostly concerned about the rural setting, which violated the three basic rules of business: location, location, and location. Gloyd sits atop a gentle knoll, an hour's drive northwest of Washington, DC. Its main street—the only street—doglegs to the left after paralleling the railroad tracks for a hundred yards. Old Victorian homes flank a quarter mile of tar and chip road lined by ancient shade trees and. At the far end of the street, the small 1878 church features a tall steeple and picturesque graveyard; many gravestones are too weatherworn to read.

Pastor Winton, who lived with his wife, son, and dog in the manse directly across the street, visited us shortly after we moved in. Many men of the cloth can be identified by a collar or vestments. Not Winston. Dressed in overalls and work boots to blend with the country folk, he invited himself in and plopped down on our couch.

"Welcome to Gloyd. Be glad to have you visit our church." He proceeded to describe a few of the more colorful characters around the area. "Your neighbor Harold is salt of the earth; will do anything for you. But don't cross his wife. She heads up the elders and runs the church with an iron hand."

"Yeah. We met him when our horse got loose and clobbered a car."

"I heard about that." Of course he had. Everyone knew everything about everyone in Gloyd. "They say you're opening a dental office; that should be interesting." No encouragement, but no discouragement either. Kate and I liked Winston and decided to attend his church. After I represented it in the USSR, the church's congregants reciprocated my efforts by encouraging me in my new business venture.

Opening day arrived with only one patient, a young family man from the church. I cleaned his teeth and Kate assisted me with a filling. Although a little rusty, she managed to avoid blowing air up his nose. He smiled when he got up. "You're an OK dentist!"

More gung ho than ever, I posted a handmade flyer on the country store's community board. It was proudly displayed amongst scraps of paper that announced newborn pups, hay, straw, and grain for sale; sheep shearer's, farriers, and welders; a brush hog and backhoe operator; chicks, goats, and rabbits for sale; and free barn cats. Several faded sheets of ruled paper gave directions to long-gone yard sales.

An old-timer went in to buy a pouch of chaw. He rubbed his sore jaw, copied my phone number, and called Kate.

"Got a tooth been painin' me for some time."

"I've got an opening first thing tomorrow morning," she offered while not mentioning that there were no other appointments. He was happy that we could see him so quickly. We were thrilled to "squeeze" him in.

He volunteered that he and his wife lived in a frame house next to the railroad tracks behind the country store. "Me an' the little woman lived in these parts fer years. Gloyd never had no dentist afore."

I had a hard time getting to sleep that night, anticipating that the next day's procedure might establish a solid reputation for me. I'd finally drifted off when a loud cacophony of barking, howling dogs drifted in through the open bedroom windows. Kate looked at the bedside clock and jumped out of bed. "Pipe down out there; it's two a.m.!" she yelled through the screen before realizing that Rusty, our mongrel Irish setter, was making the most racket.

I half opened my eyes and noticed streaks of reddish-orange flickering on the bedroom wall opposite the window.

Fire!

Bolting out of bed, I threw up the screen and stuck my head out to see if it was spreading our way. I had distasteful memories of our close call with fire on moving day.

"Do ya think anyone's called the fire department?" I asked.

"Maybe. Shouldn't we get dressed just in case?" Kate suggested.

"I guess."

Mesmerized by the flickering that filtered through the not-too-distant trees, neither of us budged. The warm glow seemed to come from the town center, a half mile away. Kate wanted to go investigate.

Not me. "If it gets any closer, wake me up" I said while crawling back under the sheets to get some rest before my morning appointment. She reluctantly pulled herself away from the window and climbed in beside me.

"I think it's pretty far away," she mumbled. I rolled over and drifted off while fire engines wailed in the distance.

Before six o'clock we were dressed and trudging sleepy eyed toward town. Stabletown Road was clogged by a traffic jam. Although a few commuters normally took the back roads to avoid rush-hour on I-270, there was never any real traffic, until that day.

"I'll bet last night's fire caused this," Kate mused as we walked past the stalled cars and climbed the hill to the country store. That's where we saw the cause of the previous night's canine commotion. A freight train from Detroit had derailed. Scores of shiny new Cadillac's, along with several railroad cars, were strewn about like matchbox cars. Trees were uprooted and telephone poles knocked over.

Bewildered commuters were trapped in the impenetrable logjam. Businessmen with briefcases wandered aimlessly, waiting in vain for a train that wasn't coming. A line had formed at the outdoor pay phone. I almost expected to see Rod Serling leaning against the country store, smoking a cigarette and describing the scene as taking place, "Somewhere in the Twilight Zone."

How is it that television crews always manage to elbow their way through the mess?

Dressed in work boots, faded blue jeans, an old flannel shirt, and battered baseball cap, I must've looked the quintessential local yokel. A buxom, blond reporter shoved a microphone in my face while her cameraman aimed his video. With a nod, her assistant flipped on his halogen spotlight and half blinded me. Behind the unnatural radiance, the pretty commentator became a disembodied voice.

"What's your name, sir?"

"Carroll," I mumbled while stuffing my hands in my torn pants pockets.

"Well, Daryl. What's your impression of last night's train wreck?"

"I was tired and rolled over to get some sleep," I muttered before announcing a little louder, "And it's Carroll—two Rs and two Ls."

You don't usually hear such lackadaisical comments on the fast-breaking, eyewitness news. And neither would I be heard. The halogen light faded as the reporter yelled "cut" and went in search of a more promising bystander.

Kate boldly stepped forward with eight-month-old Joel on her hip. Reveling in the limelight, she's infinitely more articulate than I am. The correspondent asked a myriad of questions that Kate enthusiastically answered. "The night sky filled with flickering flames. Dogs howled and…" She was showcased on the noon, six o'clock and late night news, all of which were dutifully recorded on our new VCR.

Thankfully, no one on the ill-fated train was injured. But an old farmhouse that sat hard by the tracks had been violently knocked off its stone foundation. It landed in a shattered heap of splintered wood and crushed plasterboard on Gloyd's main street. Winston announced that an elderly couple had been sleeping soundly on the second floor when it was struck. "They tumbled through the collapsing house and landed in the cellar. They're at the hospital but seem to be OK." They ended up with numerous contusions and bruises, but no broken bones.

Kate and I gazed down into the exposed, debris-filled cellar and then turned to look at the rubble trailing across the street. It was truly a miracle that the aged couple had escaped serious injury. Angels had watched over them on that fateful day. I tried to imagine the horror of being awakened by a deafening metallic screech as a train smashed into our house before we plummeted two stories through the chaos. My worst nightmares could not compare. Well, maybe that witch in Grandma's farmhouse comes close.

While stumbling through the wreckage, it dawned on me that the demolished house was once opposite the country store. The fog in my coffee-deprived brain slowly lifted as I questioned a Gloyd parishioner.

"So, Ginger. Who lives—lived—in that house?"

"The Shirleys."

"Bud Shirley?"

"Yep. Him and his wife, Dorothy." Ginger looked sad. "Poor folks. Could've been worse, though."

I stared blankly and turned introspective. *What I hoped would be my second patient is my first cancelation.* That was a selfish thought. At any rate, Bud's toothache would have to wait; he had more pressing problems.

Not only was I thankful that the Shirleys were OK, I was thankful for my wife and family. With Kate's hand cradled in mine, we slowly walked home while the rising sun of a new day chased away the surrounding mist and warmed our souls.

I extracted Bud's tooth the following week. It went well, and he shared accolades with friends about a competent new dentist in Gloyd. Through fits and starts, neighbors slowly drifted into our office. It was a solid beginning.

Just in time for a visit from the Russians.

Twenty

From Russia with Hope

I had just started my Gloyd practice when the Soviet Peace Committee sent their exchange delegation to the United States. In previous years that team had comprised a handpicked elite but it now included a steel worker, an elementary school teacher, a plumber, a carpenter, and two low-level managers. The quintessential KGB operative, thinly disguised as another teacher, was easily identified by his shifty eyes and arrogant bearing. They were all still card-carrying Communists.

Unlike my team's sojourn in the USSR, these Bridges participants stayed in private homes around DC. The KGB guy did board at St Albans with Jamie, who never let him get away with any revisionist, propaganda BS. Rural Gloyd proudly welcomed two of the intelligentsia: a dentist and an economist. Art, an elder at Pastor Winston's church, and his wife, Mary, a spitfire country girl, opened their home to them.

Leila was a financial expert on North America who worked closely with President Gorbachev. Slender, of average height with short brown hair and blue eyes, she was stylishly attired and pretty, except for her severely crowded teeth. A dentist notices that sort of thing. Having several times traveled to the United States and Canada, she was well-versed in Western customs.

Yuri, on the other hand, might've been mistaken for blue collar if not for his advanced degree and lofty title: Chairman of the Moscow University College of Dental Science. Middle-aged, he was tall and wiry with chaotic patches of thinning gray hair that never looked combed. His hesitant English smacked of a crash course.

Although their schedule was strictly controlled by the embassy, it did allow free time. There was nothing scheduled for Yuri and Leila's first day so they could recover from jet lag. I made a fun suggestion. "Hey, Art. Let's cruise the country roads so they can look around."

Yuri took my proffered cowboy hat and hopped in the back of my pickup. Not wanting to look like a spoilsport, Leila climbed up beside him but refused Kate's hat. Yuri grinned nonstop while bouncing through the countryside. Leila, a city girl, just grimaced, maybe because her hair kept blowing in her eyes. The hat would've helped.

After Leila had cleared her throat of bugs, they spent the rest of the day on our farmette. Yuri wanted to ride a horse; he sat cockeyed and beamed while I led him around the field. Leila merely tolerated Kate's horse. After dismounting, she spent a lot of time brushing horsehair off her clothes.

Yuri was a lover of antiques. Art informed him that there was an antique store "right 'ere in town." Although it was an easy walk, Yuri wanted another ride in the truck. Leila had had enough of dirty truck beds and stayed back with Mary.

"Downtown" Gloyd was a motley assortment of old buildings: the antique shop, which used to be the train station; a country store run by Koreans who could almost speak English; an auto repair shop for American-made only (no metric tools) and the post office, which lacked a bathroom for Dosia, the postmaster and only postal employee other than Art. A cardboard sign on the counter (Back in Fifteen Minutes) meant she'd gone home to take care of necessary business.

With great expectations, Yuri strode confidently into the antique shop, glancing up when the little bell on the door jingled. But his smile soon faded. Picking up an old farm implement or some other knickknack, he'd study it for a second, frown and then put it down.

"Where antiques?"

"Everything in here is an antique, Yuri," I explained.

"Just old junk." From where he stood, he was right; in Europe, antiques can be centuries old. We didn't stay long.

A couple days later, we ventured into the nearby suburbs—in my car, not the truck. Leila shook her head in disbelief at all the neat, modern homes. "This is just a showcase to impress us." Cosmopolitan Leila, only familiar with the glitter around US convention centers and convinced that destitution reigns throughout most of our country, probably thought the neighborhood was a Potemkin village.

"Yes. There's poverty and homelessness—more than we'd like—but not everywhere," I tried to explain. "My grandparents were extremely poor, even by American standards. But we have opportunities, such that I could become a doctor."

"You are a rich dentist. Most Americans live in squalor." Leila was adamant.

"Actually, most are middle class. It's true, some are filthy rich and some are dirt poor. But those are extremes."

"Not so. We have newsreels. Homeless peoples everywhere. You just show best." It was one of the few times that Yuri allied himself with Leila. Prejudices, fueled by a closely manipulated media, were hard to dispel.

"How about this? We'll go anywhere you like. You tell me where to turn." My offer seemed to intrigue Yuri. *What if the capitalist isn't bluffing*, his eyes asked.

Although Kate and I own a few acres, our house is average. It's bigger than some and smaller than many. But to the Russians it seemed palatial.

"Many peoples—families—live here?" Yuri had asked the first day.

"Just me, Kate, and the three kids." And after they visited my mom's townhouse ("No, she doesn't live with us."), and my brother's Pyleton home ("Neither does his family."), it slowly dawned on them that I might actually be telling the truth.

Any dog, but especially a big one, is a status symbol in Russia. And we had three: two rambunctious litter mates and the patriarch, Rusty. Leila squealed with delight when they jumped on the couch to snuggle with her. Yuri, however, thought we were just showing off.

While touring DC during their second week in the States, I got lost, which is not hard to do in Washington, even for natives, and inadvertently wandered into a neighborhood of ramshackle homes. Seedy-looking people sat on decaying front stoops while bored youths hung out on street corners. I quietly locked the car doors. "This is one of the poorer sections of town, so you take precautions."

Leila chimed in from the backseat. "This is exactly what we see on our news. It's everywhere."

"Our media also focuses on America's crime and social problems. But that helps us correct them," I countered. "And it's not everywhere. I'll still go wherever you want to." Although they seemed puzzled at how open I was, I think the wall of distrust was slowly crumbling.

Leila spoke up: "Can we go to a Kmart!"

"Yes, I hear of Kmart," Yuri enthusiastically echoed.

On a sunny afternoon, before our conference at Hood College, we stopped at the Frederick megastore to experience its "magic." They wandered around like kids. Yuri's mouth stood agape. He was amazed at the variety and quantity of goods on display. Even Leila seemed overwhelmed, having never seen anything like it. There weren't many big box stores near the plush downtown hotels where she normally stayed.

It all suggested that Soviet media reports of endless shortages in America might not be completely true. The novel *1984* came to mind. If the lie is big enough and repeated often enough, the masses will believe it.

Sporting goods, however, gave them pause. They stared bug-eyed at the myriad of guns for sale.

"Anyone buy?" Yuri queried.

"Most folks. There are background checks for criminal records and they are age-restricted. But if nothing is found, it's not a problem."

"People in America can shoot anyone they want to," Leila calmly told Yuri.

"It does happen and too often. It's one of many problems that we're trying to work out." On quick reflection, I decided to explain target shooting. "I was captain of my high school rifle team when we won the state championship." I grinned proudly. "I can show you my rifle when we get back."

"Nyet," they nervously exclaimed in unison.

Leila wasn't interested in buying anything; as a privileged apparatchik, she could get goods unavailable to other Russians in Moscow. Yuri, however, announced that he needed AA batteries for his camera; he was taking a lot of pictures.

I looked at the checkout line. "We'd better get going. We're due at Hood soon, and I've got extra batteries at the house."

"Nyet. I buy myself." Proud Yuri was used to waiting in long lines for a stale loaf of bread or fatty slab of beef. Relative to that, the Kmart line was moving pretty fast. They looked shocked when an impatient customer in front of us started making a scene. "What the hell's taking so long?"

But soon it was our turn. Yuri stared at the pimple-faced, gum-chewing young girl with orange and green hair at the cash register. When he finally placed the shrink-wrapped AAs on the conveyer belt, she yawned, blew a bubble, and scanned the bar code. "That'll be three dollars and fourteen cents," she mumbled.

Carefully gauging the adolescent's immaturity, he straightened up to appear even taller than he was. Squinting menacingly at the chubby little thing, he boomed with authority, "I give two dollars!"

"Huh...what?" The no longer bored cashier had stopped twirling her hair. "That's three dollars and fourteen cents with tax," she repeated.

"Nyet...No! Two dollar fifty cents. Final offer!"

Flustered, she lightly stomped one foot and stammered, "I...I can't do that, mister. It's three dollars and fourteen cents." All nearby chattering ceased as people craned their necks to see what was going on.

Not to be dissuaded, Yuri raised his chin with a haughty air. "I demand speak owner," he loudly announced.

That gave me pause. *So, just who is the* owner *of Kmart?* Leaning toward me, Leila whispered, "Are all American Jews like this?" Flabbergasted, I said nothing. I didn't even know that Yuri was Jewish—never thought about it. Obviously, bigotry had not been eliminated in the worker's paradise any more than it had been in America.

The young gal shrugged her shoulders, re-scanned the package, and pointed at the computer screen. She looked desperate, her eyes pleading for help.

"I have money, Yuri. I'll be glad to—" I offered.

He cut me short with an aristocratic wave and glared at the teen. "Let me speak boss? He know two dollars fifty cents good price."

As the line grew ever longer and folks more irritated, Kate spoke up. "We'll pay the difference, Yuri." Maybe embarrassed by this offer from a woman, he slammed a five-spot on the counter. While impatient shoppers looked on from behind, he carefully counted his change—twice.

More livid than embarrassed, Leila refused to interpret for him at the Hood conference, which was a big problem for Yuri whose English was poor at best. *I'm glad she didn't buy one of those guns.*

Yuri asked if he could see an American dentist—me—in action. Although Leila had no desire to hang out in a dental office, she came along. Maybe she felt bad about shunning Yuri at the college. As he bent over my shoulder to watch me work, she paced.

"Most of our restorations are bonded," I explained. "Anterior crowns are all porcelain so they look nice. Kate has a couple up front."

"I like see." Yuri had gold fillings that showed.

"OK. I'll get Kate when she's not busy at the desk." While I finished with my patient, Yuri dug through his coat pockets and found a small clear box containing several Soviet drills and cutting disks. I looked carefully at them; the shafts weren't exactly straight and the holes in the disk drives weren't centered. *These things probably cut with the steadiness of a flat tire.* He was very proud of them.

"Do you mind letting Yuri see your Dicor crowns?" I asked Kate while showing her his drill collection.

"Sure," she said and smiled skeptically. Kate half opened her mouth and whispered to me. "Only give him a mirror." Nothing sharp!

Yuri and Leila were scheduled to leave a couple weeks before Thanksgiving. So Gloyd Presbyterian decided to celebrate with an old-fashioned turkey dinner a little early. It would be a fun send-off. Kate and I crammed the quintessential card tables, TV trays, and folding chairs into our unfurnished living room, which also covered up the grease spot from Halfway Dick's motorcycle. About thirty neighbors squeezed in.

Before blessing the meal, Pastor Winston related a brief history of this American tradition:

"In the darkest days of the American Civil War, President Abraham Lincoln called for a National Day of Thanksgiving to remember our many blessings. It was a time when Americans were killing each other by the hundreds of thousands, yet he felt it appropriate to give thanks to our Creator, who should be remembered during the bad times as well as the good."

Leila and Yuri listened intently and respectfully bowed their heads during grace. Our small rural community had made an impression about the true source of America's ideals. We would also do well to remember, as President Lincoln had wished. Thanksgiving was the perfect ending for our Soviet guests' visit.

Not long after Yuri and Leila's return to the USSR, the entrenched Russian dictatorship began the unprecedented process of peacefully dismantling itself. Communism simply does not work.

The Berlin Wall fell.

The Sunday following that momentous occasion, Pastor Winston commented on our historical exchange with the soon-to-be former Soviet Union. He humbly complemented the congregation on successfully hosting its two citizen delegates. "I'd like to believe that our little country church was responsible for taking one or two bricks out of that terrible wall." My eyes moistened. I was thankful for the opportunity to have played a tiny role.

Epilogue

My exchange visits with the Russians are not the end of the story; they're little more than the beginning, as the reader will discover in my second book, *The Whole Tooth*. As both of my practices grew, I hired more employees. Some were efficient, some fun, and some just plain weird; I like talking about the weird ones. And periodically, some wacky individual would drift through my office door. My country practice in Gloyd, surrounded by livestock, freely roaming pets, and stray varmints, set the stage for many more bizarre events.

And more flashbacks to my Nealy Ridge childhood will further explain why I used my dental skills in overseas missions. Those villagers—lost in time—were so similar to my family and their neighbors up on The Ridge. Superficial appearances and cultural differences don't mean a lot to those eking out a harsh existence from the land. Our son, Joel, accompanied Kate and me on one fateful trip. His pale skin, blue eyes, and light-blond hair were a curiosity to adults and children alike. But he was gladly welcomed into their homes.

A simple brown envelope landed on my desk one day about a year after the Russians had left. I usually toss bulk rate mail in the trash bin, but, for some reason, I opened it. It promised exciting journeys to do dental work in rugged, poorly chartered regions around the world. Not long after I got that envelope, one life changing mission proved nearly fatal and was—.

Oops…gotta go. Rusty, our vagabond canine, just threw up an entire partly digested groundhog on our bedroom carpet. So much for not allowing animals inside our home…

Acknowledgements

Fifty years in the making, this book depicts a life that has been a joy to live. That's not to say it's been all fun. It hasn't. But the valleys combined with peaks make life worthy. It would not have been so without family and the many friends who accompanied me along the way. And I trust that none have been offended by my retelling. I wouldn't have included those zany capers if I didn't think so highly of them.

My lovely wife has been a loyal companion through this journey. As my anchor and most honest critic, she promoted those stories that should be told while omitting others for the sake of propriety. Her constancy during the many hours I was absent in spirit is an example of true devotion. I'm more in love now than when we started.

Kudos to our kids who persevered through one strange childhood. These tales weren't possible without them. I read several rough drafts out loud, even when they didn't want to listen. They made faces: "You're not really going to write about *that*, are you Daaad?"

I shamed several friends into reading my early meanderings. They had to wade through some pretty murky waters, and I do appreciate their perseverance: Harriet, Stan, Steve, Pat, Susan, Wendy, and Gail.

My editors, Helen, Barbara, and Melissa had not only many things to change in the way of punctuation and spelling, but also in clarity of thought and sentence structure. I can almost hear a groan as they realized that I don't know the difference between a winch—a rotary cable device—or a wench, a lady of the evening. Oops, spell check doesn't pick up everything.

I offer my eternal thanks to everyone who has entered my life to make it what it is today and what it will be tomorrow. Not only this book but also my chaotic journey would've been impossible without them.

And finally, but really foremost, to my Creator with whom all things are possible.

Made in the USA
Middletown, DE
28 February 2015